# QUOTES HEARD AROUND

"This hit middle-class Black people in their gut. Simi Valley was [...] every suburban county in the country, and Rodney King was our Every man. Now there are Black people all over the country, saying, 'Oh my God, what can I do?" --Roger Wilkins, College Professor

. . . . . . . . . . . . . . . . . . . . . . . . . . . . . . . . . . . . . . . . . . . . . . . . . . . . . . . . . . . .

"The rebellion was a good thing. It was a great protest saying that the day has come when if you touch one of us we're going to get one of you. Before we were too passive; we will now be more violent. In order to survive." Brother Lumumba, Consultant, New York City

. . . . . . . . . . . . . . . . . . . . . . . . . . . . . . . . . . . . . . . . . . . . . . . . . . . . . . . . . . . .

"My world had stopped. My life came to an end for awhile. From that time on, work was insignificant to me. It was as if my mother and father were fighting, and there was noting I could do." Monte Easter, L. A. Sales Representative

. . . . . . . . . . . . . . . . . . . . . . . . . . . . . . . . . . . . . . . . . . . . . . . . . . . . . . . . . . . .

"I threw my hands up last week. Here I am doing the right thing, running a business, obeying the law. I believe in the Constitution. But I've been accosted by the police coming out of my own factory. White people won't ever look at us eye to eye as equals. Norwood Clark, L. A. Businessman.

. . . . . . . . . . . . . . . . . . . . . . . . . . . . . . . . . . . . . . . . . . . . . . . . . . . . . . . . . . . .

"The verdict removed the pretense of justice. So many times we've been told, 'just be patient, the system will work,' that what we experience isn't real. This lifted the veil from that and exposed it." Dr. Medria Williams, Clinical Psychologist, L. A.

. . . . . . . . . . . . . . . . . . . . . . . . . . . . . . . . . . . . . . . . . . . . . . . . . . . . . . . . . . . .

"It had to happen. It's the only way you can get the attention of the white man." John Jackson, businessman (Dental Laboratory), L. A.

. . . . . . . . . . . . . . . . . . . . . . . . . . . . . . . . . . . . . . . . . . . . . . . . . . . . . . . . . . . .

"It was overwhelming, the sadness. I felt angry that this was the second time I felt my community was being sacrificed while providing a wake-up call to America. I won't be able to look at myself in the mirror every day if I felt the sacrifice was in vain." Clive Kennedy, a Clinical Psychologist, L. A.

. . . . . . . . . . . . . . . . . . . . . . . . . . . . . . . . . . . . . . . . . . . . . . . . . . . . . . . . . . . .

""The whole idea that people in South-Central should behave themselves so as not to embarrass people like me is ludicrous. They were right in their indignation over the lives they have been dealt by society." Leroy Bobbitt, Lawyer, L. A.
. . . . . . . . . . . . . . . . . . . . . . . . . . . . . . . . . . . . . . . . . . . . . . . . . . . . . . . . . .

"If the Kurds stood up against Saddam Hussein, the U. S. would applaud them. But somehow it's not legitimate for us to rise up no matter how bad things get." Shaka Ali, Businessman, L A.
. . . . . . . . . . . . . . . . . . . . . . . . . . . . . . . . . . . . . . . . . . . . . . . . . . . . . . . . . .

"The people who beat the truck driver was a mob. The people who beat Rodney King were public officials. In principal, if the truck driver had 25 cents and somehow could have gotten to a pay phone, he could have called 911 and gotten help. If Rodney King had a bag full of quarters in his pocket, he couldn't call 911 because it was the cops who were beating him up." Adolph Reed, a professor of political Sci.
. . . . . . . . . . . . . . . . . . . . . . . . . . . . . . . . . . . . . . . . . . . . . . . . . . . . . . . . . .

". . .Black owned, I felt a little ashamed. I thought , 'I'm using this to protect my business while they (Koreans) had to suffer. By putting the 'Black Owned' in the window, it looked like I was condoning or participating in the riots. I didn't want them to think that. So I've been extra nice to them since then." Dr. Raymont Johnson, A Dentist, L. A.
. . . . . . . . . . . . . . . . . . . . . . . . . . . . . . . . . . . . . . . . . . . . . . . . . . . . . . . . . .

"White people are not used to being the victim. Regardless of whatever we do to each other, it's not supposed to happen to white people. It's like they're saying, 'we're above all of you.  " Actor, Wesley Snipes, L. A.
. . . . . . . . . . . . . . . . . . . . . . . . . . . . . . . . . . . . . . . . . . . . . . . . . . . . . . . . . .

"What happened to Rodney King could happen to me at any time. I don't have 'physician' written all over my car. There are so many land mines out there for us. If they can get away with that with a video tape, what chance do I have as a Blackman with only lumps on my head as evidence?"
. . . . . . . . . . . . . . . . . . . . . . . . . . . . . . . . . . . . . . . . . . . . . . . . . . . . . . . . . .

"I was filled with rage. Every time I heard a Simi Valley juror I wanted to shoot the radio. It feels so awful to feel I have no value in this society, that I'm expendable. I have a good life, a nice house, I'm happy. And if I'm feeling this level of rage, what must they be feeling in South Central?"

# RODNEY KING AND THE L. A. REBELLION:

## A 1992 BLACK REBELLION IN THE UNITED STATES

*Analysis & Commentary By*

*13 Best Selling Black Writers*

## Published By

**U. B. & U. S. Communications Systems**
**1040-D Settlers Landing Rd. ● Hampton, Va. 23669**
**1-804-723-2696**

**FIRST EDITION ● FIRST PRINTING**
**JUNE, 1992**

ISBN# 1-56411-036-2                    Y.B.B.G. #0033

**Typesetting: KIM FINNEL**
Printed in the U. S. A. by
UNITED BROTHERS GRAPHICS & PRINTING UNLIMITED
P. O. Box 5368 ● Newport News, Va. 23669
1-804-244-7639

# CONTENTS

## DEDICATION

To the Memory of
*Addie Mae Collins, Carol Robertson, Carol D. McNair, Cynthia Wesley, Yusef Hakwins, Mack Parker, Emmitt Till and other Black men and women who have been wantonly murdered & brutalized in the Spring of their Lives by lowlife, racist dogs, in these United States of America: 1555 to 1992,*

*&*

*For those Great African Men and Women who fell on the battle field of injustice, while in direct service to the noble Cause of the Black Nation, we pray the strength of your strength will fortify our commitment and resolve to remain steadfast in our service to the Cause for which your life was lost,*

*& Also,*

*This book is dedicated to all those innocent Black men, women and children who in born; lived and died in oppression, many of whom never even knowing the nature of the oppression, or the nature of those holding them in subjection.*

# ACKNOWLEDGEMENTS

First of All, we acknowledge the presence of Allah in our Nation; and we acknowledge the importance and impact of the teachings of His Messenger, The Honorable Elijah Muhammad. For without the teachings of Mr. Muhammad surely no one in the Black community of Los Angeles would have been prepared for the turmoil that cut off almost all services to the area. Moreover, with the teachings of Mr. Muhammad, we are blessed to have the means and the will to bring forth this work.

We want to thank and acknowledge the great brothers and sisters who responded properly to our challenge to write and submit their reports within a one week time frame: Thank you Del Jones (our fearless War Correspondent); and we probably would not have moved as expeditiously, as we did, had it not been for the receptivity and totally positive response to our request by Steven Whitehurst, Marva Cooper, Barko Khalifah (Gregory X), Mar-Yoi Collier, Sister Reda Faard Khalifah, Al-Hajj Idris A. Muhammad, Lula B. Edwards, Munir Muhammad, Gloria Edwards-Taylor & Ahmed Hakim.

It is with a great degree of satisfaction that we introduce this publication to you. It was on April 29, 1992 that the now infamous Rodney King, "not guilty" verdict ignited the most explosive revolt in the more than 400 years old liberation struggle of African people in the United States of America.

This publication is a part of our (the contributors) response to the challenge that reverberated throughout Black America, as we witnessed the powerful expression of our dissatisfied people in Los Angeles, and elsewhere. As we eagerly followed the gripping news about the revolt, as committed, independent journalist, the thought occurred to us, "What is the strongest way that we can pro-act in the face of the blatant miscarriage of justice?" We clearly understood why our people re-acted as they did. It was also clear that we were being challenged to "do something"about this particularly detestable, blatant act in the collective face of our Nation.

No one knows better than us about the day to day existence of Africans in the U. S; how we all, in order to survive, must ignore instances, situations and many times open acts of injustice, both against us, and members of our nation. Of course most of us ignore the acts because we are disciplined enough to wait for a more opportune time to respond; while the worst of us ignore the acts because of our cowardice and acceptance of the status quo in U. S. society. Since these responses are the extreme

8

ends on the same pole, so to speak, there will be more in the middle (the masses) than there are on the ends. It is the masses that are regularly referred to as the "Sleeping Giant." We are acutely aware that the most powerful thing we can hope to do, as journalist, is to induce this sleeping giant to pro-act to news & information in his own behalf.

We also have a good degree of understanding about the fact that whenever an event happens that impact on the Sleeping Giant, causing him to move, whether he re-acts, or pro-acts will be determined by the veracity of the information; and the analysis & commentary he receives about said event. For us conscious Africans in the business of news and information, of course our objectives are to present only truthful news and information. On the other hand, we intend to present analysis and commentary about the news & information in ways that will cause our people to pro-act: meaning, act positively to the particular event in ways that will further the aims and objectives of our struggle for freedom, justice and equality. The strongest impediment to our success in achieving this objective, today, is our inability to present the information and our analysis & commentary in a timely way. The prevailing challenge we face is to get the information, and Black point of view into the marketplace of ideals as soon as possible.

Seldom do we get the first word out about an event such as the recent Los Angeles Rebellion, or any other event that happens in or out of our community. It is not because we do not have the information. Or access to good Black points of view. But since there are less than a half dozen (6) daily Black owned newspapers in North America; only one t. v. network, and relatively few Black owned radio stations, the media are simply not there to get the first word out. Though our chances of getting the first word out are slim, getting the "second word" out can be fairly certain. The "second word," as used here refers to analysis and commentary on a particular event. The *second word* is more or less the kinds of reporting that tells things about the main event. These things could be about aspects that led to the event; or about aspects that resulted from the event. In either case, this is basically the place where all Black owned media in the U. S. A. stands. Our media periodicals are primarily *weekly, monthly, and bi-monthly, etc., reports that are made after someone has already reported on the information about the event. Or events.*

Though it is very important to report on news events as they are happening (the first word, which, basically, should be good, solid facts), the second words could well be just as, or more important. The second words out, the analysis & commentary on the event, is absolutely the most important if one is to impact on the long term character by which said event is recorded as history. The Second Word is even more important, if one intends for his interpretation to clarify the truth; to influence or to solidify the gains that may have derived from the event.

For example, *what does our War Correspondent, Del Jones see and want our people to do as a result of the L. A. Rebellion? What does Sister Reda Faard Khalifah have to say about the rebellion? What does Mar-Yoi Collier, Marva Cooper, Barko Khalifah (Gregory X), Lula Bee Edwards, Steven Whitehurst, or Munir Muhammad (one of the foremost defenders of The Honorable Elijah Muhammad), Gloria Edward-Taylor have to say about the Los Angeles Rebellion? With this book, you have an opportunity to read their analysis & commentary, in a book that we aim to have in print, and before the public before any other on the Rebellion.* If not for the timely publication of this book, our people would have to wait until someone less gifted, committed and/or independent to get this kind of teaching on the subject.

* * * *

I pray that you understand very well what we shared above because most of it was written in order to make our point crystal clear: This book came into being because we presented a challenge to some 20 Black writers, coast to coast, to present a paper on the rebellion within seven days after our request. They were given a short time frame within which to respond because our main objective was to publish the first book about the Rebellion.

As we hope you agree, the ones who met the challenge not only jumped at the opportunity, the contents of their articles says clearly that they were not taking an *objective* view about the rebellion when we called. Meaning, they were not keeping up with the rebellion as simply a good news story. But were identifying the rebellion as a part of a long time struggle to rid ourselves of the stigma of oppression. They were asked to write essays as a means to express their concerns by *doing something about how the rebellion made them feel (commentary). And it's importance to African people (analysis).*

The contributors happen to be, for the most part, young gifted Black writers who have independently published their own books. Others have been, or will be published by United Brothers & United Sisters Communications Systems. Their representation does not come from every city where the rebellion spread to; this is partially because writers in the affected cities did not respond in time for inclusion in this First Edition, or were not ready when the call was made. Still others, of those who *did* respond in time, are not writers by profession. My dear cousin, Lula B. Edwards, who lives in the middle of the conflict is a case for this point. Though not a writer in the strict sense of the word, she is extremely intelligent, conscious and happens to live in the very midst of where the main action took place. She told me over the telephone: "The smoke was so thick when I came home, I couldn't find my house. I had to find another way to get home."

Though we did not have correspondents reliable enough to call on in every city, we believe you will agree that we have a enough, important representation from different regions to insure that the reader will not miss the purpose for the publication: *An important effort to take control of the means by which African people get news and information about self and kind; and events that impact on their lives.*

Please read and enjoy with the ideal of sharing your own feelings, which if you are so inclined, please send them to us as soon as possible.

Peace,

H. Khalif Khalifah, May 10, 1992

# OTHER BOOKS BY THE AUTHORS

**ADIB RASHAD:** Aspects of Euro-Centric Thoughts: Racism, Sexism, and Imperialism

**Marva Cooper:** . . . . . . . . . . . . How Beautiful De Swatches

**Ahmad Jakim** . . . . . . . . . . . . . . . . . . . . . . . Black Exodus

**Steven Whitehurst** . . . Words From An Unchained Mind

**Gloria Taylor Edwards** . . . . . . . . . . . . . The Proclamation

**Al-Hajj Idris A. Muhammad:** What To Do If Yor Are

. . . . . . . . . . . . . . . . . . . Arrested Or Framed By The Cops

**Reda Faard Khalifah** . . . . Editor *Your Black Books Guide*

**Gregory X** . . . . . . . . . . Exploring the Issue of Reparations

. . . . . . . . . . . . . . . . . . . . . . . For Black People In America

**Munir Muhammad** . . . . . . . . . . . . . . . . Business Manager

. . . . . . . . . . . . . . . . . . . . . . . . of the C. R. O. E. Report

**Lula B. Anderson-Edwards●** . A Correspondent For UBCS

**Ras Mar-Yoi Collier** . . . . . . . . . . . . . . . Ed. Your Tidewater

. . . . . . . . . . . . . . . . . . . . . . . . . . . Community Paper

**H. Khalif Khalifah** . . . . . . . Story of Two Uncompromised

Blackmen in the United States: Brother Lumumba Odingo

. . . . . . . . . . . . . . . . . . . . . . . . . . . . . & Bumpy Johnson

**Del Jones: Way Correspondent** . . . . . . . . Culture Bandits

. . . . . . . . . . . . . . . . . . . . . . . . . . . . . . . . . . . . . . . .

U. B. & U. S. COMMUNICATIONS SYSTEMS

1040-D Settlers Landing Road

Hampton, Virginia 23669

**1-804-723-2696**

14

# THE COMING TO AGE OF: 'Knowledge Is Power, Ignorance Is Death'

## By Sister Reda Faard Khalifah

NEWPORT NEWS, VIRGINIA

The Honorable Elijah Muhammad, quite a few years ago, said that there would come a time when the caucasian would come fully out of the closet and show himself, literally, to be the devil that he is. In other words, the diabolical crimes that he (Caucasian) has been perpetuating against Black people for hundreds of years would come to its full zenith, where the horrible acts that are committed would be taking place right out in the open. As openly as they were committed during chattel slavery.

The only difference being that the slaves were totally defenseless, due to an evil master plan that was carried out from 1555 to 1619, known as the preparation for the abject slavery to follow; we were forced into total submissiveness and made totally subservient to a strange and alien people who came from Europe, known as Caucasian people, who subjected us to the worse treatment ever known to a human beings.

Now, back to 1992, think about eight (4) racist, Caucasian policemen, simultaneously, continuously and unmercifully beating one (1) prone, single, poor, helpless Black man with those horrible night sticks, right out in broad day light while millions of people watched, horrified (Thanks to a local citizen's video camera). I mean, just how much more open can it get? And, to top it off, these animals made jokes and bragged about what they had done!

I have to give credit where credit is due. The Honorable Elijah Muhammad was absolutely right. This Caucasian is doing exactly what he (The Honorable Elijah Muhammad) said that he would do. Evidently, this Caucasian feels that since he has been getting away with this kind of conduct against Black people for so long, that there is just no need to ever sneak around again and make feeble attempts to cover up his devilish acts. After all, who's going to punish him any way? Certainly not his own kind.

But wait! There is a new day on the horizon. Black people

Are fighting back. We have finally gotten literally sick and tired of all the injustice that we have endured for going on five (5) hundred years, at the hands of this so-called White man. We will probably never know for sure the total number of caucasians that were killed by our retaliating people. The authorities confirm but five, but we know that scores were pulled from autos and whipped.

Also, a group of warring gangs put aside their differences and came together in unity -- to pool their resources and strength against their real enemy, which is the enemy of all Black people. We are truly in a new day and time.

What is responsible for this new show of unity among Black people? Well, for years, many of us have been reaching out and teaching our people that '**Knowledge is power** and **Ignorance is Death**.' The truth is, we have been **dying** in record numbers since we were kidnaped and brought to these shores against our will. We have been murdered in more ways than the *rational* mind could ever dream of. Knowledge tells us what we have done, and what we can do about it. From this knowledge will come the wisdom to act in our strongest best interest.

After fear was deliberately branded into us (man, woman and child), by forcing us to witness the initial, cold blooded murder of our fore parents...this fear, along with not being allowed to learn how to read or write, and after separating us from our parents and relatives so that they could not teach us any correct knowledge about anything, including ourselves, paved the way to our complete and total **ignorance** of our true name, language, religion, history and culture.

Since then, we have continued to allow these things to happen to us because of our ignorance. So what is **Ignorance**....if not **Death**?

**Knowledge is Power** has been a long time coming among the ranks of our people. But it is on the scene today. It is making us see what our natural enemy has always had in store for us. And it is **not** '*Freedom, Justice and Equality.*' It is now, as it has always been, '*Slavery, Suffering and Death.*'

We all know that now. There is no more guessing. No more doubt. Whether we all admit it or not, we **know** it. Only a retarded type of fear would keep us from admitting it.

We should really take a good look at what's happening in Los Angeles The murderers of our people who wear the big guns and badges are, ironically, becoming confused. The badge that gave them so much faith and confidence in their ability to kill Black people at will and get away with it, is not working anymore. They will think twice before they break in on someone again with their guns drawn and bullets flying. From what I understand, they may go in shooting, but they will surely go back out on a stretcher. In other words, what's good for the goose or, as my brother Malcolm X once put "It's just a case of the chickens coming home to roost."

**Knowledge** is what is bringing this about, plain and simple. Correct **knowledge** of the time in which we live. **Knowledge** of **God, Knowledge** of the Devil, and **Knowledge** of the Black man.

We know that in Unity there is strength. And as long as we keep Allah (God) first, by understanding that He is indeed with the righteous, and that He has control over all things, and we continue to unify as a people while praying and depending on no one but Allah to help us fight successfully, when necessary, and win our battles whatever the adversity. Then we will truly be victorious as a unified people.

Look out world! The Sleeping Giant is finally awakening!!

Remember, We Must Read!!

Peace.

. . . . . . . . . . . . . . . . . . . . . . . . . . . . . . . . . . . . . . . . . . . . . . . .
**SISTER REDA FAARD KHALIFAH** is the Editor-In-Chief of YOUR BLACK BOOKS GUIDE, a publication published by U. B. & U. S. Communications Systems, the family business developed by she and her husband, H. Khalif Khalifah. She was born in Roanoke Rapids, N. C. but has lived in the city of Newport News, Virginia since childhood.

Sister Reda is one of the foremost writing proponents for preventive (wholistic) health. As the former Executive Editor of The National Newport News & Commentator, she has written dozens of articles that promoted the use of natural healing herbs as the surest way to the maintenance of good spiritual and physical health.

She resides in Newport News with her husband and three children: Tamureda (10), Alike (8) and Nadirah (4).

*The Following is an edited copy of the lead story in **The National Newport News & Commentator; Volume 10 Number 67: MAY, 1992***

# THE SLEEPING GIANT

# MOVES IN US IN L. A.

## 58 Dead; 5000 Injuries; 8000 Arrests; $1 Billion Property Damage. . .

**By H. KHALIF KHALIFAH**

After more than 25 years of seemingly dormancy; a period in which any number of notorious cases of murder by police, and other open, hostile acts of oppression against them, including literally hundreds of thousands of young Black men, rounded up and thrown away in high tech (and low tech) prisons (see related story on page 8), coast to coast, the so-called "Sleeping Giant" (the Black, Unheeded, masses) appear to have awakened with a vengeance.

Black Youth in Los Angeles, chanting the war cry, *"No Justice, No Peace,"* heard in Howard Beach Bensonhurst, the Bronx, (in NYC), and Boston, Mass. etc. have led a thoroughly mixed population in three days of a rebellion that spread to some two dozen other cities in the United States of America.

# "THE RISING TURBULENCE IS ORIGINAL BUT STILL ARGUES FROM THE CLASSICAL SCHOOL OF THE BLACK STRUGGLE"

Kendryck V. C. Allen, from one of his books, "*The Psychology of Color and Racial Sexual Behavior.*

As we go to press, Los Angeles, San Francisco & Atlanta, Ga. are burning in varying degrees of flames. States of emergency have been declared, as the mayors of the cities imposed " dawn to dusk curfews." Other cities in rebellion are being added to the list, even as we write. .

And as they have during past rebellions, by African people in the U. S., the national, caucasian leadership appear to have *suddenly* discovered the awful conditions, and actual, pitiful state of the Black communities. Taking to the same air ways that was used during the 1980's, & '90's to wage a relentless,  open attack to take back the gains made in the 1960's, the Bush Administration have charged it's top, so-called "Law Enforcement Officials," the Attorney General, FBI, etc. to speed up an investigation into the brutal beating of a Black man that occurred, and was broadcast to the world over 12 months ago.

### SINGLY PRAISE FOR OPEN ENEMY OF BLACK PEOPLE

As is well known, the beating of Rodney King by Los Angeles cops was recorded on video tape and broadcast

Repeatedly, not only in this country, but worldwide. Also, in the aftermath of the beating, the Chief of the police in L. A., a fellow named Daryl Gates, was investigated and found to be "out of control" in a contract with the City in which the Black mayor, or no one else had any authority to hold him accountable for a record of 20 years of systemic police brutality in general, but particularly when it comes to Black people in the city of Los Angeles.

Of course an uproar was heard, nationwide, about the King beating; the Black community was frustrated because of the failure to rid itself of an abusive police chief. To rub it in, according to the Rev. Jesse Jackson, *"two weeks after the King beating, that Mr. Bush, himself said he was sickened by, the U.S. Chiefs of Police had their annual meeting in Washington, D. C. During the meeting at the White House, Darryl Gates was singled out for special praise by this same president."*

Mr. Jackson's comments were made during a CNN (Cable News Network) broadcast in which the Interviewer had subtly implied that Jackson may be using the Black Rebellion in L. A. "for political gains."

Prominent Black leaders coast to coast are speaking out in terms never seen in the history of our oppression in North America. And though they, for the most part, are only echoing the open remarks and declarations by the "Unheeded People," as young Black writer, Ken-dryckAllen, a Graduate student at Temple University in

Philadelphia, calls the Black Youth in his recently published book, **"The Psychology of Race and Color."**

As per usual in a national crisis with the Black community, the caucasian owners of the broadcast networks were careful in their choice of Black politicians and experts to analyze and make projections about the rebellions (and what they portend). Mr. Benjamin Hooks, Julian Bonds, and of course Rev. Jackson, etc. was the strata of leadership seen nationwide, including on the only Black owned network, Black Entertainment Network (BET). The likes of Minister Louis Farrakhan (The Nation of Islam), Imari Obadele (The Republic of New Afrika) , Munir Muhammad (C. R. O. E., Coalition For the Remembrance of Elijah) and any number of other independent Black men were not heard from (on national t. v.). But fortunately, the Black community is not as easily fooled as they have been in past generations: so even as the U. S. cities burn, the words, acts and deeds of these men, and the forecasts & prophecies of past giants whom they represent, or are ideologically akin to, is providing the underlying base and, in some cases, justification for the frightening Black Rebellion of 1992.

Kendryck Allen's book, and dozens of other "best sellers" in the Black Books Movement, have already, clearly, analyzed the deteriorating condition of African people over the past few years. The rebellions are eerily manifestations of many of their predictions about what

24

Would result from the open attacks on all of the major, for the most part, symbolic gains Black people were making in the U. S. before the advent of Nixon, Reagan and George Bush. Many predict in graphic detail that one day the "Unheeded People" would be fed up with oppression to the point that they would react in ways that oppressed people have traditionally *proacted*.

"We were not expecting too much to begin with, but to release them after the video taping of a brutal beating is more than the people would take," said a young Black man in California, during a telephone interview on the day after the acquittal of the four cops.

"I hope this wakes up our people; people have to start waking up, he continued. "I really hope this is a shot that will be heard around the world by all African people. We must do for self. . ." This young man declared that he was going to redouble his efforts to awaken African people through his Black Books business.

As I must conclude this article in the midst of broadcast indicating that the rebellions are increasing and spreading in all directions in the U. S., many of the written words of Kendryck V. C. Allen are being manifested like a book of prophecy:

*"The state of mind of the Unheeded People in America is definitely worth examining. These people would over turn this system without hesitation because they have absolutely nothing to lose.*

*H. Khalif Khalifah is the C. E. O. of U. B. & U. S. Communications Systems, the publishers of Your Black Books Guide, The National Newport News & Commentator & Your Tidewater Community Paper. He is also the author of six books, including PROFUSION: Analysis and commentary on the Impact of The Blackman's Guide to Understanding the Blackwoman, How to Publish & Distribute Your Own Newspaper, Magazine or Book, The Legacy of The Honorable Elijah Muhammad, The Brief Affair, and The Story of Two Uncompromised Blackmen in the Slavery Society Called the United States of America: Bumpy Johnson & Brother Lumumba Odingo.*

*Brother Khalifah lives in Newport News, Va. with his wife and three children, Tamureda, Alike and Nadirah. His son, Gregory X (Ibn H. Khalif Khalifah) also works in the family business. "*

# IMPRESSIONS:

# AN EYEWITNESS REPORT

## Written
## by

# LULA B. EDWARDS
## Los Angeles, California

"Wasn't that terrible what happened in Los Angeles last week?" yes, yes it was terrible but what's worse is, that it had to happen at all. It's terrible white Americans say *why* and African Americans say, "*I don't understand?*" The answer is you can't see tomorrow when today doesn't cross your mind. You can't find tomorrow when you have lost yesterday. From the blue print of institutional racism to the roadways that guided it to the systematic oppression of its people -- it had to happen.

We are faith filled, non-violent, giving and forgiving people by nature. Lets be very clear and specific about who was out in the street: young, old, Black, White, Hispanic and Asian. This is bigger and broader than a Black/White issue, it's a humane issue, have and have nots (economics) -- humane.

Rodney King is not the first man to be beaten and abused by authorities; only the first to be video taped and beaten to the degree that he was; and no one punished for the crime.

We are disrespected by actions, words and deeds daily. The actions have been played and replayed until it has become a mind set, a way of life - natural, natural to them inhumane to us.

If we were the animalistic people we're portrayed to be, we would have rioted after the beating. But We said *"No, the system will work."* Then authorities blatantly tell us we didn't see what we saw. And the jury used this as a transparent ruse to excuse brazen brutality. . . Why did we burn down our own community? Because we didn't have anything anyway. We live here, but what is burned down, we didn't own it anyway. Can't you see, we have a better chance of owning it now than we ever would have, as it was before.

Yes, some Black businesses were also destroyed. Some because in war, whether mental or physical, there will be casualties. Others lost their businesses because they forgot who they were. And the ones with the fire, knew they had forgotten. In the natural realm, just as it is in the spiritual, when you know whose you are you know who you are. We forgot how each one teaches one. Once upon a time, These things kept us stable and rooted in our culture. Years of disparage, desperation and degradation have turned your 1000 points of light, Mr. Bush, into Los Angeles' 1000 blazes. *"Why didn't we talk with someone."* We've been talking - nobody listened.

—We've been beaten in the streets. Our rights are illegally and *judiciously* taken away in the courts - nobody will listen. What are we supposed to do? America would have us go meekly away. But we refuse to go. So now, what are you going to do. Better Question: What can you do that you have not already tried? But tell us, what are you going to do. Tell us now, while we have your attention -- the whole world is also watching and listening.

— This eruption had to happen. Progress comes from change - we had to give it a push. Yes, if we have to, we will give it another push. But we would rather have peace. The peace that comes with justice. We believe in Peace when possible - violence when necessary, **No justice, no peace.**

### THOUGHTS & OBSERVATIONS

1. No one has addressed Rodney King's plea to stop the violence. It has been said that he was emotional, shy and caring. All these things are true but he was also scared (as he nervously rubbed his arm and seemed to duck or jump when a helicopter went overhead).

No one seemed to notice that Rodney appear to have a problem with his jaw, tongue and speech. Unnoticed also was what Rodney King seemed to be repeating, (something obviously programmed in him), about having his day in court; and it not being over...

• No one has mentioned that Rodney now has emotional and psychological problems. It is also not widely known that Rodney had to be sedated after he heard the verdict.

2. Black Females said they "didn't know Rodney was so attractive." We hadn't seen him for a year; so the only picture we had seen of him, was the swollen battered pictures taken at the time of his arrest. Of course, we have seen the video tape of the four cops beating him, but he was laying on his stomach most of the time.

3. One of the things cited that could help our community and nation immediately, would be to close up crack houses. America needs to blow away the smoke screen and attack the real issues. Stop playing games.

• Several months before the King verdict a Korean woman shot and killed 15 year old Sister Latasha Harlin in the back of the head as she was leaving the store after putting orange juice on the counter. Korean lady received 5 years probation. This too was video taped.

Get real, Blacks don't bring the drugs into America. We aren't in control of it. Stop it from coming in and you won't have crack houses. Most of our legitimate businesses fail because we can't get distribution, so we aren't distributing the drugs.

Because of the very real fear of the drug issue the new crime Bills are taking away our basic rights, which are supposed to be guaranteed under the Bill of Rights. Opinion polls say over 78% of the people said they would forego the right of having warrants for search and seizures because of the drug problem. This is scary to me! Wake Up! The Drug laws were originally meant for the large Cartels or drug lords, not the brothers on the corner. It's not like they don't know where these people are. The brother on the street is being swept up and given time that don't fit the crime (disparaged in sentencing). Not just with drug crimes, but across the board). Federal sentencing starts at 10 years with no parole. Brothers getting 10-20 years with no drugs found in possession, no money or equipment found in their homes or on their persons.

. . . . . . . . . . . . . . . . . . . . . . . . . . . . . . . . . . . . . . . . . . . . . . . . . . .

**LULA B. ANDERSON-EDWARDS** was born in Gosport, Alabama. She has lived in South-Central Los Angeles, California for more than 20 years.

# THE RODNEY KING RIOTS:
## Revolt or Revolution?
### Written
### by

## STEVEN WHITEHURST

## author of the highly acclaimed book
## WORDS FROM AN UNCHAINED MIND

**WHAT IS A REVOLT?**
**WHAT IS A REVOLUTION?**

Before beginning this analysis I feel that for the utmost clarity, I must first give a brief definition of terms. In my thesis statement a question...a comparison, between revolt and revolution is made. I feel that it is of paramount importance to start by establishing a working definition of those terms.

A revolt is a spontaneous action, or group of actions, by a group of people who are acting--many times through violent means--to change a particular condition, present at the time.

A revolution is also an action, or group of actions, taken to effect change...but on a broader, more complete scale. A revolution may be initiated by a revolt, but it grows out of dissatisfaction, not with a particular condition, but with conditions in general. For that reason, where a revolt might be set off by a severe act of abuse, and might for a period of time utilize violent means to effect change, its lasting effect is negligible due to its spontaneous nature, and its lack of direction, discipline, focus, and clearly established long-range plan to bring about systemic change. Revolution, on the other hand, has a very visible, lasting effect due to its on-going, structured nature, and because of its commitment to long-range, wide-reaching, radical change.

With the definitions of these two terms firmly established, you, the reader, will understand why--during the course of this essay--I use one in place of the other. Revolt--and its related terms, such as rebellion or uprising- and revolution, while being similar in some ways, are different in many: thus, their results are different. With that being said, let us begin. . .

From the earliest days of the African Holocaust--where Black people were kidnaped from their homeland to become victims of murderous European exploitation--to

The present, people of African descent have been rising up against their oppressors. Here in Amerikkka this spirit of rebellion has shown itself numerous times. From the sea based uprising of Joseph Cinque and the land based revolts of Gabriel Prosser, Denmark Vesey and Nat Turner, in the 1800's, to the rebellions across Amerikkka's blood-soaked landscape (Watts, Detroit etc.) in the 1960's, the lack of political, social and economic justice was at the root. Each episode of African revolt can be directly traced to lack of empowerment and equality in Amerikkka's racist, repressive system; a system shaped and run by a wicked, treacherous government, who's claim to historical fame is being the greatest -- continually growing -- collection of liars and genocidal vandals ever to stain the face of the earth. In a system where a person is victimized -- whether through de jure slavery and apartheid, or de facto systemic discrimination -- due to color of skin, political, social and economic empowerment is denied. Just such a system has been imposed on Black people in Amerikkka.

As a result of this nefarious system, Black working class people have acquired a distrust of, and dislike for, the U.S. Government and its promises of just treatment. Feelings of despair, hopelessness, helplessness, betrayal, and outright rage abound in the Black community; and it was this pustule of total discontent which came to a head and exploded in each of the aforementioned revolts. But because these acts of insurrection had limited scope and

34

effect, they are placed in the category of revolt and remain in the pages of history as minor sparks in a highly flammable garbage dump of a system that should've been incinerated at its inception. A revolt, while it does have the proper energy, just doesn't have the necessary range to do the job . . . **but revolution does!**

By definition a revolution can begin with a revolt, therefore the same elements of ignition are present in both. With that being said, the most recent period with the best environment for revolution was the 1960's. With movements for change crossing race, class and gender lines, the atmosphere for total societal correction was evident. The Black community, with its great agents of liberation -- agents such as Malcolm X and the Black Panther Party--in place, and the emotions and conditions being what they were, was a powder keg set to blow. The U.S. Government was aware of this fact, and true to fascist form, turned to its domestic military arm ("law enforcement") to crush the threat. The police, with their pistol and whip mentality, came into the Black community like an invading army of murderers, occupying the area much like a foreign troop occupies territory. The paid assassins came in and commenced with their bloody war to destroy African freedom fighters. Two casualties of this war were Fred Hampton, Deputy Chairman of the Illinois Black Panther Party, and Mark Clark, a member of the party from Peoria, both of whom were murdered in cold blood by a police death squad, on Chicago's Westside, on

December 4, 1969. On a connected but larger, more covert scale the U.S. Government's Federal Bureau of Investigation was also busy in its mission-employing a variety of means -- to destroy any exponents of Black liberation. The FBI's COunter INTELligence PROgram had the following as its goals: *1) Prevent the coalition of militant black nationalist groups, 2) Prevent the rise of a messiah who could unify, and electrify, the militant black nationalist movement, 3) Prevent militant Black nationalist groups from gaining respectability, by discrediting them to the community, and 4) A final goal should be to prevent the long-range growth of militant black nationalist organizations, especially among youth.* The government was successful and the forces of African liberation were eliminated . . . but the elements that caused their rise were not. That brings us up to the present.

## THE RODNEY KING BEATING

After the March 3, 1991, police beating of Los Angeles motorist Rodney King, and the subsequent acquittal of the storm troopers by a jury showing Amerikkka's true face, violence erupted on this country's streets during the week of April 25, 1992. The sad-but-true fact is that Rodney King's case is neither the first, nor will it be the last to exemplify the lack of social empowerment and justice for African people in Amerikkka. The lack of political and economic empowerment is shown in the statistic, that since the Gary Convention of 1972 -- when Black "leaders"

36

sold the political soul of Black America to the Democratic Party, and to the racist two-party system in greater sense -- the number of Black elected officials has risen by over 300% while the poverty level of Black people has risen by over 400%. What that shows me is, Black elected officials can improve neither the political nor the economic condition of Black people due to their ties to a system which was built on the exploitation of Black people. It is most clear to me that if one goes into a beats belly willingly, expecting that beast to show mercy and to allow him to climb back out, that person will only again see the light of day as a lump of digested and discarded waste. The fact of the matter is, there is neither justice, nor equality, waiting for Black people in this country. When you have a president like George Bush who stereotypes African people as criminals -- as he did with his use of Willie Horton during The 1988 campaign -- and then, with the support of a bipartisan legislature, sends those same people to their deaths in a hypocritical, imperialist war for oil in the Persian Gulf, than its easy to see how Amerikkka and its racist government feel about justice and equality for Black people.

It's safe to say that with the smoke over Amerikkka thinning, and the number of confrontations with the fascist pig cops lessening, the recent unrest can be named "The Rodney King Revolt." Without a revolutionary paradigm to direct it the recent explosion of African rage -- in large part -- was unleashed in its own community, rather than on the "powers-that-be," and consequently will go into the history books as another one of those little sparks. But, it's also safe to say that the same conditions that caused this revolt, and those before it, will eventually lead to an African Revolution!

I, myself, am more an advocate of African electoral -- rather than violent -- revolution. It is my feeling that Black people, once removed from the racist clutches of the two-party system, and organized into an independent party which is Black-led and built on the Black Agenda, can effect major change. But anytime racist aggression is brought against the Black community, then the Black community is justified in taking up arms and defending itself **"BY ANY MEANS NECESSARY."** The agents of governmental oppression are still present in the communities of working class Africans, as are the elements and conditions that gave rise to the previously mentioned revolts. The fact of the matter is, the African people of this country, either by **"THE BALLOT OR THE BULLET,"** will achieve freedom. Be it electoral or violent, there will be an **AFRICAN REVOLUTION !!!**

* * * *

*STEVEN WHITEHURST was born in Chicago, Il. on March 3, 1967, the product of a single-parent family. He spent his early childhood years growing up in the housing projects of Chicago's south side, before moving to Harvey, Illinois, where he graduated from Lowell-Longfellow Junior High School (1980) and Thornton Township High School (1984). After Spending a brief stint studying at Southern Illinois University at Carbondale, he went on to earn his A. A. in history (1987)* and his A. S. in geography (1988) from Thornton Community College (now South Suburban College), graduating with high honors.

He received his B. A. in history (1990) from Chicago State University, where he also minored in political science. In addition to graduating Cum Laude, Steven was selected for inclusion to Chicago State's Deal List (1989 & 1990), Chicago State's Vice President's List (1989) and to the National Dean's List (1989 & 1990). During his collegiate career he was the recipient of eight different scholarships and academic awards. He is a member of the Phi Theta Kappa National Junior College Honor Fraternity (Psi Pi Chapter), Outstanding College Students of America, and All-American Scholars. His writings have been published worldwide, and his poetry earned him the New Scriblerus Society's Creative Excellence Award in 1988. Politically he has worked as an Election Judge, a Volunteer Deputy Registration Officer, a canvasser and political organizer during numerous campaigns, a Media Coordinator for an Illinois "Gubernatorial Candidate " and he has held two political offices.

Steven's first book, **WORDS FROM AN UNCHAINED MIND** was published by U. B. & U. S. Communications Systems in the fall of 1991.

# LOS ANGELES MAY, 1992-STEPPING-STONE

## by
# Marva Cooper

### Lynchburg, Virginia

APRIL 4, 1992 LOS ANGELES, CALIFORNIA 58 DEAD, 2300 INJURED, 7500 to 18,000 ARRESTED AND 1 BILLION DOLLARS IN PROPERTY DAMAGE. LOSSES IN GOODS AND SERVICES NOT CALCULATED

For nearly one week the city of Los Angeles has reeled and rocked following the jury decision of NOT GUILTY in the case of Rodney G. King, an African-American man whom video film showed was beaten by four members of the Los Angeles Police Department. While one must wonder if Kings' case was truly administered by his peers, a cause for even deeper pondering is what is the *heart condition*, or the thought perception about the situation that precipitated the rage, which in this case was the brutal beating of Rodney G. King. What motivated twelve people to unanimously decide they did not believe what their eyes saw. These and other issues will be addressed as this article continues.

While a vast majority of all Americans felt the finding of the four police officers in the King case of not guilty was a miscarriage of justice, we must examined an old and extremely formidable foe of all Americans; Institutionalized racism. Indeed racism has plagued this country for countless generations. The book entitled: INSTITUTIONAL RACISM IN AMERICA, edited by Louis L Knowles and Kenneth Prewith states; "It is often said that the law is the foundation of society... For most Americans the legal system works fairly well. The written standards of conduct and the police apparatus is set up to enforce them are established and administered by persons with interest and perspectives similar to those of the majority of white America. But for those who differ substantially in economic status or culture from the white middle class, the apparatus breaks down...We emphasize the racism of the legal structures themselves because it is more basic than (even) personal racism of administrators, thus has more profound implications to change (advances in destroying racism)."

While these thoughts were penned in 1969 - and strides of progress has been made since then, the revolt which burst out in Los Angeles now certainly all America should redefine the commitment to a united purpose of equal opportunity and justice for ALL Americans.

All Americans can exercise the right to get involved with changing institutions which perpetuate injustice, unequal opportunity for all persons. Let it become a proven fact that diligence, hard-work and dedication can succeed and bring positive change.

Find out what your representatives at the federal, state and local level plan to DO about urban upliftment. We can march for peace and pray for peace but until we attack the root of the problem we'll keep staggering under the oppression of racism or dwell with the Damocle(ic) sword of possible destructive situations as we just witnessed in Los Angeles. The wise man once said a "house divided can not stand." Each person in this country is involved from one aspect or the other, therefore each plays some role in the uniting or disuniting of America.

It was a terrible thing that those who participated in the violence, destruction and mayhem wrecked so much havoc on themselves and the city. Certainly anarchy IS NOT the answer. Yet, it is all too obvious that those who resorted to destructive action felt no sense of connection whatsoever to the whole of their city. While lawlessness must be condemned for obvious reasons, concerted efforts need to be made to foster hope in persons who must live their lives (for this moment) within the confines of the lower social economic group within urban America. Governor Clinton of Arkansas stated; "Millions within our inner cities have lost contact with the values and aspirations of the rest of the country."

This writer suggest millions within our inner cities have NEVER had contact with the values or aspirations of middle America! Many only know grinding poverty and the eking out of an existence in the midst of crime, personal deprivation and fear for family and self. We do not need a clinical psychologist to tell us what these circumstances can do to one's mentality. Morals/character may be viewed as a small sacrifice when a persons survival is threatened. Was it not once said of the man Job, 'Skin in behalf of skin, everything a man has he will give for his soul.' Everyday millions of urban dwelling Americans face these choices! We as individuals must ask ourselves, given the same circumstances, and living conditions 'How would I react?'

Empathy, will not excuse negative social conduct but, it will put one in the others place, which can become the impetus for all to work towards the positive goal of insuring that opportunities for justice and success exist for all. For many persons caught in the evil clutches of poverty, they feel their plight is largely due to race. Few have the time to give much thought to *not* being academically prepared to compete (many for reasons ranging from finance to abuse simply could not educate themselves). Then there have been examples where persons allow themselves to get caught up in what appears to be hedonistic pleasures which often leads to a further strain on already limited resources, possible damage to health and more frustration. It would be easy indeed to roll this other America off the tongue in criticism yet, what affects this America will ultimately affect the other.

## WHY NOT CLINICS TO FIGHT RACISM

*Why not form Clinics to Combat Racism all across America?* These clinics are necessary, for racism is a social disease and it's time America treated it as such, for it is as deadly as AIDS. The staff of such clinics would consist of psychologist, educators, social workers, representatives from the community and any persons who could make a positive contribution from writers to biologist! These clinics would have a rotating board of directors who WORKED in and as liaisons to help people have knowledge of their feelings and thoughts which have motivated them to act or not act. People of all races would be welcomed and given the opportunity to 'talk it out.' It would be well to encourage all persons considering jobs as public servants to serve an internship living, for a period of not less than thirty days under the precise conditions of those whom they would serve. For example, any person wishing to administer the law such as an attorney, corrections officer, educator, social worker and of course politicians should be required to live for a period in the Black community. There's no way one can administer anything that is needed for the people unless one knows to some extent whom one is dealing with!

Living in a 'hand to mouth' situation, experiencing the short term inconvenience of waiting in long food stamp/welfare lines, health care lines as at a clinic in most large cities and being aware of the long term effect of existing on the bitter edge can have a powerful catharsis effect on the spirit. It is people who give life to racism; it is people who can destroy it. Whether one is a victim or perpetrator is largely a personal choice.

A thought provoking, indeed state of affairs, is when those who break the law are the ones in the forefront, attracting attention to the plight of what has been called the other America, the downpressed. It is not the decent and hardworking poor men and women of urban Africa America which labor under poor health care, lack of finances to mention a few problems, who have by their lack of a voice, been able to solicit aid to their harsh existence but the ones expressing that Armaggedonic mentality.

May we all resolve to create a social renaissance - death to racism through re-education and dedication establishing the reality of positive urban planning, encourage all regardless of social position, 'take advantage of your right to vote! 'Approach your policy makers with ideas concerning education, health care and laws. Let us make it a goal to ask self, 'what have I done for humanity today?'

Let's make the memory of April 29,1992 a stepping stone for a positive present and future better relations for all Americans. After all what is the present and future but a condensation of the past evolving towards infinity, A united America?

* * * *

*MARVA COOPER is a writer of short stories for children and adults, lyricist, stage performer, lecturer, conductor of creative writing workshops, producer/host of a cable-television program, a traveling story-teller fashioned after the griots of Ancient Africa, with a modern twist and a visual artist who uses the medium of fabric.*

*Sister Marva's first book of poetry, **How Beautiful De Swatches**, was published by U. B. & U. S. Communications Systems in 1991.*

Bibliography

Washington Post, Sunday Edition May 3, 1992

Institutional Racism in America
copyright 1969
Edited by: Louis L. Knowles & Kenneth Prewith

# LOS ANGELES AND THE LAWS OF POLITICAL DEVELOPMENT

## By
# Del Jones,
## The War Correspondent

**PHILADELPHIA, MAY 5, 1992**

Somehow, they missed the kente cloth we were rapped in, they missed the X-Caps, dashikis and colorful material dancing on our women's rounded hips. They read it all as Afrikan profiling with no substance, just a fad some would say.

They viewed it all as window dressing adorning our old political mentalities, yeah just new wrapping for the same old hamburger.

It was just another "official corner side ass kicking" meted out to yet another Black victim. Sure it was captured on film but so was the fiery death in Philly of the MOVE family. Everyone tipped toed away from that terror, that carnage, that murder. White supremacy

47

believed we were dead from the neck up and mere perpetual victims of their hate.

"With their Global Genocide in full effect, they felt all they had to do was to continue to herd us into place." Their physical and psychological abuse of Black people would continue, they thought, because we were asleep at the wheel in a vehicle they knew could run over them with the right drivers. They were wrong, dead wrong!

Their social scientist, bureaucracy blunders, political punks, police terrorists and corporate thieves slipped into a comfort zone awaiting the genocidal death planned for us from inside "think tanks" of the insane. These capsules of white fantasy has sold white supremacy the notion that we will just slip into death, viced by Crack and AIDS.

Ignored were the indicators that shouted "Afrika!" Total disregard for the tattletale culture of Afrikan people that is the true barometer of the political direction of our people globally.

But especially in the motion of the Afrikan domiciled here in the belly of the beast (Amerikkka) were clear signs that "The Po' can't Take no mo'"

Never, I repeat never can the political laws of development be ignored. Whites feel that because we are captive in their foul gut, that we are not a nation but a disjointed, brainwashed reactionary people. They believe that Madison Avenue, Television, athletes and entertainers, control our political motion or lack of motion. They really believe that they have us down to a science, when in fact, we are more unpredictable then ever.

Unless, it is understood that we function with the laws of political development like any other nation, all outsiders view as the Afrikan personality will only confuse them.

*of*

— The first stage of political action of the oppressed is the nonviolent petitioning of those in power to lighten up and relieve the suffering. The second stage is organizing the people (women, youth, workers, students, professionals, etc.) to speak collectively to the needs of the oppressed Third stage is the executing of positive action activities to the left of the consciousness of the people, staging crippling strikes (general strikes) to bring complete work stoppage and economically punish the system for not responding positively.

The fourth stage is collecting people power to develop political power within the system (that delivers very little). The fifth stage is recognizing that the political leadership is working with the enemy in cooling out the people, faking representation and creating neocolonial situations. This stage has Black faces fronting for white supremacy, while betraying the people and ushering in a more brutal form of repression (Mayor Wilson Goode v. Move Kenneth Gibson v. Newark's Black Community, Mayor Maynard Jackson and the Atlanta Killings).

Their jobs is to oppress, confuse, cover up, and fake us out. They are our Mobutu Sese, our Daniel Moi, our Eric

Williams, and Papa and Baby Docs. Without them every blow thrown at the enemy would land flush and tear the roof off the mothersucker.

Chocolate middlemen they are, in the way of direct hits against the enemy, while confusing the people. Fronting as if they represent progress, when in fact, they represent a step back to total rule. Fuzzy contradictions are missed by the people and naked emotionalism is used to involve them in the con game.

If you think my analysis breaks down in the 70's you are wrong. For now, we must stir in their mass media attack which delays positive actions, confuses our people, misrepresents history, distorts the news, delivers a pale barbaric white value system to the victimized and brands a Hollywood manufactured reality into our sizzling brains. A reality that has the victims paying millions to worship their icons such as: Disneyland, GI-Joe, a pale Jesus Christ, assortment of cops, lawyers, soap opera fantasies and macho images of the barbarian.

On our side of the tracks we also receive those same images in Black face as Eddy Murphy, Damon Wayans, Danny Glover, Gregory Hines and other lead our perceptions away from our culture and dead into their's.

On the musical front they offer Michael Jackson, Baby Face and Prince as positive role models for young Black men. In addition young Black girls are led to believe these type are the best of Black manhood. What a choice, What a choice! To nail the trap shut, they project Hammer, Kid

'N' Play and Jazzy Jeff and the Fresh Prince as the top of the line hip-hop artists. While running vicious lying propaganda programs on the powerful Professor Griff, formally of Public Enemy, Sister Souljah, X-Klan, Bran Nubians and Public Enemy among others.

They even twist the young arms of Public Enemy and KRS-ONE to record with their children (Culture Bandits) or support their integrationist theme's Yelling anti-semetic this 'n-semetic that, they threaten the cash flow of weak artists like these and win. We must supply back for the young warriors or they will be turned against each other and be destroyed. Those loyal, like Professor Griff and Souljah must be rewarded with our respect, support and protection.

All of this looks like a well oiled brainwashing machine destined to deliver a warped consciousness to our people, while setting them up for the kill.

The effects can never be underestimated, our consciousness is crippled just by being in their polluted environment. The result is that we are always involved in remedial work in a life and death struggle for the consciousness of our people. In short, we don't control the information and image diets of our people, therefore we wrestle with the oppressor for their very sanity.

Yet somehow, some way, our people will not go down, and they continue to reach for Afrika, our-story, family solidarity and true liberation. This strength is what scares

51

the hell out of the barbarians as they move toward a final solution.

Having set up all of that, let's move on.

If it were not for their demonic mass media expertise, we would have kicked their ass and moved on long ago. Consequently, they continue to perfect their media's mental attack on our developing consciousness. This attack has bought them time. When it looked like they would not get out of the 70's trap of Vietnam and internal urban rebellion from Afrika people, their mass media saved the day and bought them the time to get up off the deck and take an automatic eight count.

Understand me clearly, the next stage should have been organized guerrilla warfare that would have brought this country to a halt. It would have crippled the means of production as rail yards would have been disrupted, utilities would have been attacked and destroyed, airports, interstate trucking, shipping facilities, and hit and run armed struggle would have led to a rumble like the world has never seen.

Instead they used their athletes and entertainers to fan out across the country, tricky pacification programs like OIC and the Job Corp., Model Cities and assorted federal and corporate funding programs that made maintaining poverty profitable to our traditional leaders like SCLC, NAACP, CORE, PUSH and local operations of pro-poverty Anti-Poverty Programs. Do you understand what I'm saying?

Traditional leadership has been co-opted and turned at the heart of the liberation efforts of our people. For example, non-violence was a tactic not the goal, the goal was freedom. They institutionalized it into a goal...pretty good trick huh? we have freedom + you

As I said under stage one of the "Laws of Development," non violent petitioning of those in power is jump street. Here in Amerikkka they created a whole beachhead, under Martin King's name. this enabled them to lock too many of our people on "stage one" no matter what the realistic was happening to us in society.

Only by using the mass media could people be given a belief in the "invented reality," while not recognizing the death, destruction and decay all around them.

Ever since the 60's those who control television programming have known it was their job to give a fantasy version of police work and how it relates to justice. It was their job to drive impressions into the people's consciousness that was not earned on the streets by the system's first line of defense.

In the 60's it was "Mod Squad" and "I Spy," with Bill Cosby, that made domestic and international traitors look heroic. Cosby has been riding on that for years. While in fact he was playing the dirty spy, the real C.I.A. was engaged in delaying decolonization of Afrika, assassinating Afrikan leaders (like Patrice Lumumba of Congo). While domestically Clarence Williams III was promoting that a police infiltrator of Black Community

53

groups were cool. A double edge sword but just the beginning.

Shows like "Dragnet" and "Adam 12" dealing with the Los Angles Police Department was a joke to those from L. A. who felt the bone crushing nightsticks, life sucking choke holds (now supposed to be outlawed) and body piercing bullets.

Now, action programs of real police work saturate the tube in shows like "Cops, Rescue 911 and Top Cops." This is the media back drop, which led to the clash between reality and their invented reality that blew the lid off of L. A. and its after shock waves rippled across this country and into Canada.

Don't get me wrong, I'm not saying we've only been tricked and psyched into a passive response to neo-slavery, we have also been assassinated, imprisoned, hounded out of the country, coerced, starved, while some even punked out. The Counter Intelligence Program of the FBI is well documented (Cointelpro). In addition, all police forces had their 'Mod Squads" to infiltrate disrupt, frame and destroy Black organizations. And it all worked well to slow our roll, scatter our troops, deliver lack of confidence in the movement among the people among the people and the buy the time the system needed to regroup.

Malcolm's chief of security was Gene Roberts an FBI informant, who later testified against the Panther 21 in New York. The Assassination of the dynamic Fred Hampton and Mark Clark in Chicago was the collective work of local and national intelligence units and on  and on.

Ya see, Riot is an oppressor's word, it has no rhyme or reason its just an outburst of the uncivilized. It attaches no blame to those who set up and maintain a system of exploitation that is so brutal that it destroys life. The mass media of this cowardly nation throws it around like a dirty garment for the oppressed whenever they take matters in their own hands...don't put it on. L. A. like  Watts, like Detroit, like Newark, like Attica Prison were uprisings against the vicious oppression heaped on the heads of the powerless.

Obviously, the struggle is between civilized  or barbarians as we travel deeper into the 1990's. Their invented reality and "media thought police" will not hold the tidal wave of suffering that crashes against their fragile dam of lies daily. The poverty, deprivation, police brutality, government produced drug environment and the biochemical warfare (AIDS) has chipped away all illusions. Sprinkle on the video tape confirmation (Rodney Kings whipping) that we don't supper from mass paranoid and the ingredients for the Los Angles Uprising was in place..

Our illustrious Elder and historian Chancellor Williams asked "How did we get from the pyramids to the projects. The questions of the 90's is how we gonna get back.  In recent years we have been studying, as a people, as the Black books revolution continues to unveil the truth of our-story. What we find is a reason to to be proud of the collective contributions of our people. We are also alerted to the methods of our enemies.

—We know they have used our humanism against us and have confused us into thinking cowardice is humane and non-violence is productive...nothing can be further from the truth.

Now we should be ready to talk about the recent Los Angels Uprising. It would be ahistorical to have jumped into a discussion of events without laying the ground work. We know that the beating of Rodney was video taped violence that the whole world saw. Consequently, the acquittal of these barbarians with badge has been tasted by the whole world. As a matter of fact a guilty verdict would have slowed our development.

— Too many Blacks are floating through life in denial of white supremacy and its violence against our people. Many believe, as whites pretend to believe, that police brutality is nothing but sour grapes from Black people. Therefore, two things needed to be proven were proved, the police job is to control, terrorize and oppress Black folk. The other point that was clarified was that there is no justice for Blacks under any conditions. Only by accident will Black folk gets justice.

As a communicator and an organizer, it makes my job easier when vivid examples of the oppression is demonstrated . After moving that denial away from the invented reality, it is clear that we are in hell and under the gun of our deadly white enemies. After realizing that we can move our collective problems with clear vision.

An elder asked "where were the "Skinheads," where were the KKK, where were the Aryan Nation and where were the neo-Nazi when Black people stood up in Los Angles."

Its seems that after the straw broke the camel's back everybody got outta the way of the fiery of the Afrikan Race. Yet, it was the nationwide conditions that added to the local fires in L.A.

All over the globe we are suffering from the attack of white supremacy's genocidal warfare against us. We see the dying all around us, from the dusty sands of Ethiopia to dunes of the Sudan. From the urban ruins in Liberia to the war torn regions of Angola and Mozambique, we are dying from the white boys murder or instigation. From Toronto Canada to Tampa Florida we had to make the statement " we ain't going out like that." —cypress hill

Joblessness and homelessness have our people walking around like zombies, sleeping on the street, dying in the gutter, dueling against an invisible ghost. Our infant mortality rate is the highest. Also, young Black men dropping like flies in an assortment of off times ways.

Since we are educated (trained) by our enemies, this miseducation fosters self-hatred, that when coupled with the mass media diet (radio/t.v. /film/video/music/fashions etc.) a deadly unconsciousness is developed in the victim.

The appetite for drugs, the destruction of the family, the

lack of a sense of community, and the need for gangs arise.

Gangs can be involved with drug distribution, violence of all types including drive by shootings. What should be the Black nations military might, warriors, protectors are socialized to feed on the community to one degree or another. They also take and make sure none of these negatives spill into the white world especially the world of the rich and famous.

However, with the help of the positive Rappers, the emergence of Black culture and our-story, a new consciousness has been developing under those X-Caps. From Tarzan's grip our culture has been seized and as we put it on, it demands a new behavior and response to old racist phenomena. Because, no one is as clear that genocide is in full effect like the Homeboys.

In addition the re-emergence of the political thought of Malcolm X demands a new manly posture that can't tolerate the dissing of the past. In the gun sight of white power is the Homeboy and he knows it and many are prepared to rumble for his life and the life of his people.

You think I'm romanticizing? Check this out ! After the final stats are in over 50 people have lost their lives, and over a billions dollars of damages has been done. That's a hell of a price for this broke country to pay  for four redneck pigs. In addition, if you check the rest of the cities that burned, you will note that billions were lost.

58

Listen, CIA President George Bush would not mind paying the price to check out the dissent across the nation, but he never dreamed it would hurt so much. Even if he needed an incident to help him increase financing to the Federal Emergency Act, King Alfred Plan and other like organisms of reaction, it still was not worth it.

The idea of attempting to contain a nationwide uprising with a minority army must bother him at night. What works on paper is hell in the streets. He must've been reminded that "think tanks" are just that and not reality.

Did ya see Jesse Jackson marching around with an Amerikkkan flag across his shoulder? Old tired Benjamin Hooks, Magic Johnson and Rodney King were of no assistance when the shit hit the fan. Because the people had for a moment saw reality and struck back at it.

To sum it all up, we only have to check with Ted Koppel of ABC's Nightline. He had the brothers from the street on. They slapped Ted around like the reactionary Mad Comic book looking punk he is thus shocking the nation into realizing the stereotypes of gang members were useless. The brothers from the Cripps and the Bloods gang spoke of the poor parenting that had been going on. They said the charges that the gangs were looting was a lie. "Check the films of the looting and you will find poor people, families of all races involved in that." They went on to say that they found the strong condemnation of the looting out of synch with the billion dollar bailouts of the S&L's.

Ted and probably some of you were shocked at the political knowledge of these so-called gangsters.

They also let the world know that there were specific targets of the fires. They called the burning of over 100 Asian businesses "Our Urban Renewal." And in light of the violence and exploitation by the Asians in our community, there is no wonder why they are the targets of the warriors. Also, it is important to note, that many Asians were seen firing indiscriminately into the crowds with Uzis and other illegal weapons. Let's see how many are identified on video tape and prosecuted like the brothers.

Their intellect traveled further, when they spoke on how Reagan and Bush had destroyed the social programs won from the Watts Uprising in 1965, before many of them were born. Also, they remembered the name of Arthur Mcduffie whom the police beat to death in Miami causing that uprising years ago. In short many were defenders of their community and should be respected. —"We are not looting, our thing is straight up against the pigs" was how they put it.

We must see everything "Thru Afrikan Eyes" that the other man's reality is a bullshit trap to turn us against each other in distrust and violent stupor. The white supremacist infrastructure is the target and Revolution is the goal.

Considering the laws of development, the Los Angeles' uprising doesn't constitute a revolution, but you can bet one is on the way. The whiteboy can't stop his demonic ways and the act of putting genocide in full effect means we are in a state of war. The youth on the street knows that and are preparing . Can we deliver the ideological Pan-Afrikanism our people need to negate white supremacy?

If they rumble without us they will be slaughtered, together we bring coherency to their energy, clarity to their objectives and brains to their brains to their balls...forward with the revolution.

. . . . . . . . . . . . . . . . . . . . . . . . . . . . . . . . . . . . . . . . .

**DEL JONES** is Author of *"CULTURE BANDITS Vol. I and BLACK HOLOCAUST: Global Genocide."*

# THE INEVITABLE R.O.D.N.E.Y

(R)realization (O)ppression (D)id (N)ot (E)nd (Y)et

## *A*

## *CONSPIRACY,*

## *AND CATASTROPHE*

## *TOWARD PROACTIVITY*

By

**Ras. Mar-Yoi T. Collier**

NEWPORT NEWS, VIRGINIA

We are living in a world that has evolved to a point where the actions, events, and issues of humankind are not freak mishaps. In these times, nothing happens without a reason; there are no surprises that have not been planned. Every major event, and issue facing us - humankind, is hosted by sons of men. All events and issues involve players, who are the hosts; and those being played, the masses, you and me.

In the 90's, however, some new minds have emerged in the game. These new players are of the Humankind, and have risen from the masses -- you and me. Their ability to rise was made so by the unseen Player in the game, Who has been, and is the Ultimate victor of the game, that is played in His world, His universe, and through His creations, since he/she -- the Most high God, allowed the game to begin in the beginning. Therefore, they -- the conspirators, are not the ultimate host of the game, they only control the board for a short time, and the end of this time is at hand.

The re-emerged players in the game have arisen again through new minds equipped with all that our ancestors had gained, and with our positioning in time, the *overstanding* of the knowledge given to our ancestors, through the divine intervention of the Ultimate host, can be made manifest. Today we can overstand the true story behind issues and events of the world, no longer recognizing them as mishaps to be reacted to and then forgotten, but we can realize them as plans both divine and conspired, and in doing this we can proactively choose to play our role in either the divine plan or the vain but necessary conspiracy.

To analyze the Rodney King issue, and the major events (International Media coverage of the beating, and The culminating Los Angeles Rebellion), which made it a world-wide issue, a amount of knowledge bases will have to be referred to. This is so that the issues and catastrophic events will not be seen as a mishap to react to, but as a conspiracy and divine plan being carried out that we all can proactively contribute to.

The Knowledge bases referred to will be from, biblical, Eurocentric scholarly perspectives, and Afrocentric Scholarly perspectives. These knowledge bases will offer information allowing the analysis to look at political, economic, social, and spiritual considerations behind and for the issues and events; and will guide the analysis to resolutions based on those political, social, economic, and spiritual considerations.

The plot or conspiracy against God, Nature, The World, and the most direct children of God, the children of the sun, has a long track record, traceable to the ones' called satan, since the beginning of time. However, the exact planned conspiracy that has evolved to its modern form has specific origins traceable to those first groups of white men who robbed the temples, and libraries of the children of the sun during the time when the process toward their enslavement, both physical and mental, begin. The white Roman and Greek men were the first to start the conspiracy, but it was European slave holders and capitalist who developed and strategized the conspiracy. The history of secret societies, fraternities, and groups will inform you about the existence of these conspirators. Refer to *The New World Order*, by a white scholar named

A. Ralph Emerson, The *Secret Relationship between the Blacks and Jews* by The Nation of Islam historical research group, or Terrance Jacksons *Putting It All Together*, to get in depth information about their existence and conscious purposes against God, Nature, and the Masses.

America was and is a product of all the conspirators. Its rise in the world, and role to the world put the conspirators in control like they had never been able to achieve. It was this great Nation which would deceive masses like you and me into, what I call in My first book, *Aspects of Multiculturalism* (due out this summer), the aristocrats dream self willed submission to oppression'. Aldous Huxley, in his book *Brave New World*, refers to the words of one called The Grand Inquisitor, Feodor Mikhailovich Dostoevski, which clearly voices our conspirators aims "In the end they (the people) will lay their freedom at our (the controllers) feet and say to us ' make us your slaves but feed us. ' "

America fronted a major role to the world. This being the role of standing for Truth, justice, liberty, and other democratic principles which made it easier to influence people to submit to its political, social, and economic order, which would feed us. What better way to win the masses -- the children of God, into your order than to make them believe you stand for truth, and justice, two of God's greatest attributes?

From America's rise in the World scene, the conspiracy took its most deceptive state, because it was during this time that the conspirators had to hide their true intent and purpose (in order to get the masses' dependency) The oppressor had figured out that dependency was the key to keeping the children of the sun in check. Providing peoples' basic needs, and programming their perception of needs, wants, and other drives through education would ensure the continuance of their rulership and dominance. Huxley comments:

"The older dictators (aristocrats) fell because they could never supply their subjects with enough bread, enough circuses enough miracles and mysteries.

Under a scientific dictatorship education will really work -- with the result that most men and women will grow up to love their servitude and will never dream of revolution

There seems to be no good reason why a thoroughly scientific dictatorship should ever be overthrown."

The scientific dictatorship spoken of by Huxley is epitomized and was to be made manifest in America. It needs to be overstood that scientific dictatorship is referring to a formulated way of ruling masses of people. In other words, master minds have studied man, that is the common man, you and me, and have become familiar with our ways, enabling them, master minds, to calculate a way of ruling the masses without revolution. Plato, Aristotle, Machiavelli, Darwin, Malthus, Freud, Weishaupt, and Kissinger, to name a few, are of these master minds and conspirators whose ideals and devilistic leadership would contribute and become scientific dictatorship. The full implementation of this scientific dictatorship will result in the manifestation of that written on the dollar bill (when our conspirators begin working toward their ultimate aim), and is expressed in the Latin words under the seal on the bill, NOVUS ORDO SECLORUM, which means THE NEW WORLD ORDER.

From the founding of America and The Illuminati, started by Adam Weishaupt in 1776, a major secret society of the conspirators against God, Nature, and we children of God, the conspiracy took total offense. No longer was it evolutionary from this point, most issues and events of the World were more a part of a conspired plan then ever before. Of course there were always unforeseen occurrences, but adjustment of plans, as we shall see, was no problem for our oppressors.

During this time the masses were needed for the building of this great Nation, and to carry out the implementation of this New World Order -- on their backs; until the nation could modernize to the point that it, and its interdependent nations of the world could operate. Therefore, the conspirators great task was to use us until they had enough control over the world's wealth to keep us in total check.

During slavery the conspirators did not care about forcing people of color into labor positions, but the morality of the masses, and the democratic principles caused slavery to come to an end. So the conspirators made the adjustment because total dependency of the masses on their economic system had not been achieved. The New World Order was not fully in place to operate as planned. The oppressors would have to go through industrialization, and modernization before they could keep their world control without the use of mass labor.

After slavery the conspirators were still blatant in their oppression of people of color. Other masses had still suffered from desensitivity to oppression due to witnessing the brutalities of slavery. This lessened the impact of brutalities after slavery, and was not challenged until the sixties.

During the sixties the conspirators played one of their best rounds in this game. The morality of the masses, and lessened fear, as well as repressed anger of the oppressed, caused the first real threat to the conspirators to occur during the sixties. The conspirators knew that it was too early to remain uncompromising in their oppressive nature because they still needed the labor and minds of the masses to take society to its modernized and automated state. The state of society that would allow the oppressor to rule and maintain control of the world and its resources without mass labor.

Also the masses would have to be made more dependent on the establishment. Before the 70's, or what I call the age of materialism, people were still very attached to the land and were knowledgeable enough to provide needs. Canning food, making clothes, and farming were common but the 70's would change this. Therefore, the newest element to carry their plan to it's completion was needed. This was the element by which the masses were made to believe that oppression had ended, and that America was indeed the land of the free, and opportunity. Free meaning to work, opportunity being the job both resulting in dependency.

Before the sixties America had no problem maintaining what my father in his book PHOENIX ARISING calls " Paleo-Racism." This is the form of racism that is overt and blatant in its application. This is the form of oppression where people realize and are aware of their oppression, in that they face it every day. The conspirators had no problem with this because the masses in the world had either no problem with it, or were not focusing on it. Also from emancipation to the sixties the world conspiracy was going as planned. Industrialization had occurred world wide, giving the conspirators the necessary capabilities to mass produce, a major step toward gaining control. Mass Media technology had developed, giving the conspirators another vehicle to spread their materialized ideologies. Property of the World had been redistributed. Africa and Asia had their maps redrawn. The white mans market and economic systems were launched world wide. The democratic ideal was being propagated to the world, again, for the purpose of winning over more people and nations into the white man's economic, political, and social systems. And basic control techniques for the masses of people were being tested. These control techniques being, war, and famine. World War I, II, and the Great Depression were used to test the amount of oppression that could be oppressed on the masses through the conspirators political, economic, and social systems. Communism was a move that occurred so that one nation could build up a world arsenal without other nations becoming fearful. Every major event that occurred in this century are final steps toward the New World Order. A. Ralph Epperson states:

"World wars have been fought to further its aims. Adolf Hitler, the Nazi Socialist, supported the goal of the planners. The majority of the people will not readily accept "the new world order "but will be deceived into accepting it by two strategies:

1. Those in favor of the changes will have become seated in the very thrones of power, generally without the public realizing that fact:

2. The "old world order" will be destroyed piece by piece, by a series of planned "nibbles" at the established format.

The Communist Party is actively supporting the changes for the "new world order." The tenets of Christianity, which were the base for the "Old World order," will have to be eliminated. If the slower, methodical techniques of change do not function, violence will be introduced and controlled by the planners. The people of the world will give up their freedom to the "controllers" because there will be a planned famine, or some depression or war. The change to the "New World Order" is coming shortly,

70

perhaps beginning after 1989, so that the entire structure will be in place by 1999." *||*

The sixties threatened everything the conspirators had been working towards. All over the world people of color were roaring for independence and freedom. In Africa and America the masses were on the verge of revolution, that is if they did not get what they wanted - freedom. Also the Illuminati had great fear of ' a messiah ' (Dr. King, Elijah Muhammad, Malcolm X, and Nelson Mandela) rallying people together around 'old world order' principles such as, justice, equality, liberty, freedom, peace, and love. So when the whole world was at this level of consciousness during the sixties, those who had been studying us -- children of God, knew that only a major compromise and deception would save them. However, deception was no problem for the conspirators this was a technique passed down from the Illuminati founder Adam Weishaupt:

"There must not a single purpose ever come in sight... that may betray our aims against religion and the state ('we the people').

One must speak one way and sometimes another, but so as never to contradict ourselves, and so that, with respect to our true way of thinking, we may be impenetrable." (John Robison, *Proofs of a Conspiracy*, Originally published in 1798, republished 1967 by Western Islands; New York ). This technique is applied daily by top officials, corporate heads and other power holders. Just observe your nightly news and political commentaries with a conscious eye and this truth will reveal itself.

The conspirators were aware that from the sixties they would have to make people of the world feel that all oppression had ended, and what better place to do this than America. If we the masses were not made to believe we had achieved freedom, here in America, or Independence in Africa and Asia, the conspirators would have felt the heat of their greatest fear; millions of colored people revolting. Also the conspirators realized that everyone should get a taste of the pie, so that when it (the pie, being food clothing and shelter) is taken away, people will do as the Grand Inquisator had foreseen, beg ' make us your slave, just feed us. ' Finally the conspirators also were aware that it was not quite time for turning on the "New World Order." For modernization and technology, would require the minds of the children of the son to bring about automation, computerization, and the space age.

Therefore, Dr. King and Malcolm X were killed; they knew this would have to be done to stop the resulting unity from the spread of 'old world order' principles, and that they could successfully get away with it because people were not prepared nor unified enough to carry out a successful revolution. This is the same reason Mandela was locked up, and Elijah Muhammad was conspired against. King was kept alive for sometime, one reason is because his non- violence ideology temporarily lessened

Him as a threat. A second reason is because they realized he could be used to make the transition, and create the deception that oppression was coming to an end. They felt the accomplishments of King would pacify the people by making King stand as a testimony to their readiness and willingness to " let freedom ring. " However they took his idea of freedom and redefined it to the freedom to work and be dependent on their establishment, not the freedom King meant: which was freedom according to 'Old World Order ' standards, freedom to land, freedom to produce, and thus freedom to live and express.

By the time King realized he was being used, and that there was no such thing as real truth, justice, and liberty, in America, or any other so - called democratic nation in the world, it was too late. He to was terminated. But to our oppressor he had served his purpose.

The 70's and 80's arrived and the 'New World Order' was well on its way to full implementation. We felt we were free, and that our oppression had ended. Therefore we the masses, devoted our full energies to being Americans, not knowing that we were making ourselves more into slaves like never before. The 70's and 80's moved us more into being subject to the 'scientific dictatorship.' Our taking to 'Old World Order" way's such as true spirituality which brought about a taking to, unity, peace, brotherhood, sisterhood, and other Godly way's, was replaced with a taking to 'new World order " way's, such as materialism which bought about, disunity, greed, Black on Black crime, jealously, envy, and other such way's that would ensure our dependency on things of the world, and ensure that we would come begging when they are taken away.

This time brought another attack from our conspirators through education. The 70's and 80's produced whites, in Black bodies, using the media and education. As a people, we did the worse thing we could do for ourselves, we went to sleep, and were pacified. With the children of the sun, in America asleep, the conspirators could devote there energies to some final preparations on the World scene. On the World Scene, the following major-events Played out by the masses, and planned by the oppressors were final steps toward full Implementation of the "New World Order"

Politically in the 70's and 80's the focus of the oppressors was to align all those nations which were to be independent; Vietnam, South American Nations, The Middle East, and other Nations where they didn't have a firm grip on its people and leaders such as Cuba, and Libya. With Communism playing its role as the apparent foe, America, working directly for the conspirators, could play its role of liberator. Appearing to spread Democracy, and after decades of Building up a World Arms Bank, America could successfully beat non-aligned and supposed oppressive nations in line. That is, of course in line with the World Plan that they - the true oppressors and Conspirators have been Working toward since 1776.

In 1975, Henry Kissinger, former Secretary of State and Secret Society member, was well aware of the World Plan being Worked on: "Our Nation is uniquely endowed to play a creative and decisive role in the New Order which is taking form around us!" *(Seattle Post-Intelligence, Apr. 18, 1975 p. A-2)*

Politically the 70's and 80's was also a time to test and see how much the effects of Materialism had pacified the masses. Therefore, many blatant scandals, such as, Watergate, the Savings and loan scandal, and the Iran Contra Scandal, to name a few, were carried out for this purpose. Other Injustices were committed, all serious and worthy of Mass uproar, but the effects of Materialism and greater dependency caused injustices in the 70's and 80's to receive minor protest if any. This showed the conspirators they would soon be able to finally treat the masses the way they have long sought to, and that their plans on the Social Front were indeed working the masses into' Self Willed Submission to Oppression.' Socially the 70's and 80's, as I stated earlier, was the age of materialism. In the 20's after Industrialization, and during the first age of Mass Media, whites had experienced the First Major wave of Material Culture. As I point out in my book Material Culture describes the Way of life by which external vs. Internal reality is the emphasis. Material Culture produces individuals who deal with outer reality vs. inner reality . Outer reality places emphasis on consumption, ownership, Individuality, possessiveness

("That's mine"), and obtainment ("give me"). Inner reality places emphasizes on oneness in its unified form, Sharing, and togetherness.

Dealing with Outer reality, alone, without dealing with inner reality creates norms of today such as, the Drug problem, increased crime, Greed, Disunity, result from the loss of 'Old World Order' Ways which stressed inner reality and outer reality.

As a people our focus on outer reality, increased during the 70's and 80's. Materialism was like a disease spread through T. V. Radio, Video's, Magazines, School, and 400 years of feeling we had nothing. The 70's and 80's were a time of Social Complacency to, the results of Materialism.

The Masses were almost successful in their efforts to solidify as a unit during the 60's and early 70's by striving for the Idea's which they felt the Nations stood for, but almost successful was not enough. It was as though we had made it to the mountain, and were about to go over, but on our course, our energies were redirected. For example, the protest, sit-ins, and Marches which occurred during the 60's were backed by a solidified, and energized people. The oppressor played the game well because he first created the perception that Integration was the freedom we want, and he then created the perception that we had achieved what we wanted.

Affirmative action and other legislation passed during the 60's was to make us feel as though we were effective in getting what we want. Therefore, this perception, compounded with the effects of Materialism, was like a knock out Blow, that put us out for the count, at least enough time for their New World Order to be fully implemented. Every time we tried to get back up before the count, the effects of Materialism Knocked us Back down. Think about it. The 70's and 80's was the age of Suedo Protest, Suedo Marches, and Suedo Legislation. It was as though our complacency and Materialism drained the true energy, and Drive behind Protest, making what used to be a threat to our oppressor a mere social reaction.

Socially, street life, fast cars, liquor, girls, and money was our new idea of success. Some of us become educated, and attended church, but neither of these institutions did little but keep us asleep.

Economically, the 70's and 80's was a time to also make the final shifts to the new world order. The world market was extended to the four corners of the earth, establishing the European market systems beyond the reaches that imperialism did, through the power increasing international corporations. The earth's resources, and property was slowly being re-shifted into the absolute control of governments, and international corporations.

People were made consumers more than ever before, the production self sufficient idea's kept alive on farms, and in segregated communities, was replaced with an idea of success that finalized our dependency status. This idea is best expressed in the familiar phrase,' get and job. ' No longer did we make jobs, no longer did we can food, no onger did we make clothes, our new freedom only allowed us to get a job to buy what we needed.

Economically the 70's and 80's was also a time to make inflation, recession, and depression a accepted reality. Would you believe me if I told you that inflation, recession, depression, and poverty are all man made. There is enough food in the world for everyone and their children to eat till their bellies are full. . .

So now the year is 1992. We are closer to the day's of the beast (New World Order) than ever before. The Rodney King event took many of us by surprise. Why? Simply because we didn't Realize Oppression Did Not End Yet. The facts in this article and the Rodney King event must bring about the (R)EALIZATION (O)PPRESSION (D)ID (N)OT (E)ND (Y)ET. Our response to this blatant act of oppression and New World stance against the Old World reality called JUSTICE, must be extreme, proactive, and implemented. We cannot react to this event with protest, sit-ins, or marches, nor should we continue to burn down our neighborhoods. Why? One reason is because all of those reactions were expected. As with the Marches in the 70's and 80's, the oppressor sits behind his throne looking at us Marching and singing ' we shall over come,' knowing that we are doing exactly what they expected.

The Video, shown on International T.V., the mysterious whipping out of Rodney King, the all white jury, the Black judge, the Black mayor, and the non - guilty verdict, were all planned. The result, such as the riot, could very well

78

have been anticipated to prepare the nation for the coming martial law, war on drug and crime; a.ka. , the war on coloreds. Consider it,  who would not expect a city of poor, socially angered, and deprived masses who had nothing else to lose not to get violent when such a blatant act of oppression occurred.

Since the removal of the civil rights act did not bring about the hoped for uproar to prepare the nation for martial law, a more blatant act of oppression would be necessary to move a people who had been pacified for twenty years- the beating of a black man on national T.V., and letting four white cops get away with it would and did do the trick.

Over the next few month's, crime, race violence, and civil disorder will increase. By the time George Bush, son of Prescott Bush, secret society member, who will of course be the next president, get back in office Martial law will be just around the corner. The war against drugs and crime, aka, the war on coloreds, and the socially undesirables  will make Rodney King's a daily occurrence. Be prepared for July 93',95',98', and of course 1999.

Though the days of Blatant oppression must come according to GOD's plan there are many proactive measures that we as the children of GOD are to take in order that we might make our contributions to the fulfillment of the higher plan.

The first and most important step is on the individual level. KNOW THY SELF. The Old World order was built around this ideal. From it will come the necessary knowledge to deal with outer reality realistically as well as inner reality the missing link of today to achieving true success.

This action involves reading. In that this is the last days, a.k.a, the day's of judgment, one thing which makes it so is that the truth about, man, woman, self, life, nature, and God, all are one and the same. Today however, there is nothing not known. Reading will enable you to first gain a conscious view of everything you see going on, not only in the world, but in your daily living and interaction. Act accordingly; not according to the sick mentality currently operating in most people's materialized New World minds, but act according to Godliness, and your true nature as a human. Knowledge of self and its nature is power in a world where the power holders and conspirators have created ignorance and distorted truth about the nature of self, thus resulting in its death.

Once reading gives you the knowledge base you can be on your way to your first resurrection. From here you will be equipped to operate, develop, and plan according to the truth which you now see.

The second step towards proactivity involves your assessing your capabilities first to be used for your individual physical, mental, and spiritual survival, then to see what contributions you are capable of for bring unity among other righteous seed and children of GOD.

Each of us is a leader in this struggle. Once one knows what one can do, we are then able to do it.

The third step toward proactivity is networking. Working together with your people. We must work as a people toward independence. When everything is cut off around us (food, clothing, shelter), we should have individually networked with so many people that we all have circles/groups of people whom we have developed relationships with by, which each person in the group contributes toward the survival, and development of the whole.

Networking must move toward the focused goal of consolidating all our human, and resource materials (money, land, seeds, technological resources, etc...). This each 'I' must do today so that tomorrow we all are doing it.

There is so much more, but I hope I have given you a more clear idea about King and the reality he and we face. My two final points. One, when the time comes to beg for food, don't, no matter how hungry you get, for this will result in you getting the mark of the beast. You are likely to be whatever number you use to stay attached to the system (i.e. credit cards, social security #'s, food club card numbers etc.). Begging is not to be viewed as getting on your knees, but begging is what Clarence Thomas does, or what many of us college graduates do, 'get a job' for corporate America.

Second, realize that oppression shall come to an end, but never be fooled, for it shall not be the oppressor who supposedly ends it, as we believed he did in the 60's ,but it shall be GOD working through his children. This is how we shall know. Peace.

3.     "And it shall come to pass in the day that the Lord Shall give thee rest from thy sorrow, and from thy fear, and from the hard bondage wherein thou wast made to serve.

4     That Thou shalt take up this proverb against the king of Babylon, and Say, how hath the oppressor ceased the golden city ceased!5.   The Lord hath broken the staff of the Wicked, and the sceptre of the rulers.

6.     He who smote the people in wrath with a centinual stroke, he that ruled the nations in anger, is persecuted, and none hindereth.

Isaiah 14:3-6

. . . . . . . . . . . . . . . . . . . . . . . . . . . . . . . . . . . . . . . . . . .

**MAR-YOI COLLIER** is the 22 year old  Editor of **Your Tidewater Community Paper,** He is a former Associate Editor of Black Reflections Magazine (published by his brother Maxie in Baltimore, Md.), an accomplished reggae musician; and a senior at Hampton University.

# NEXT STOP L. A.

## By

## Gregory X (Ibn H. K. Khalifah)

## Hampton, Virginia

Consider the time. To the believer in God it is self-evident just what type of times We are living in. Truly a blind man, who believes in God could see these are most strange times indeed. The Rodney King verdict and the aforecoming riots in Los Angeles, Atlanta, San Francisco and much of North America, restored sight to some who were yet blind to the times. And just what time is it? It is the time for the Black man to love, unify and do for self and take back his original position as Ruler by the Grace of Allah (God). It is the time for the caucasian white ruled world to step down voluntarily or face the chastisement of Allah. Well, just how do We know We are living in these times?

Going back to what was said earlier, white control of the planet is falling. Not all at once, but in degrees like the setting of the sun. The United States is now the largest debtor nation on earth. Only one of the top twenty largest banks in the world is American owned. The United States' education system is not in the least competitive with any of her rival powers. The United States continues to lose friends, influence and respect with peoples all across the world and must use force to impose her will. (Witness the war in the Persian Gulf, the expulsion of military bases in the Philippines and other parts of the world, the rise of Fundamentalist Islam against the West, the President with his beggar hat in his hand in Asia and the rotting and rebellious mass of humanity both on and within her borders). Sometimes though, the setting of this sun still comes so quickly that it startles and even shocks some people.

Many a white man in high places was not only disturbed, but genuinely surprised by the swiftness and boldness of violence resulting from the verdict. (Especially the devil at the highest level - President Bush, spelling it out for the weak at heart.) Just as the world was in fact caught by surprise when the German people broke down the Berlin Wall and seemed to unite overnight. Just as the Communist Eastern European nations and even Russian governments fell and split violently apart. All of their money spent on spies, analysts and experts could not or did not warn Presidents Reagan and Bush of the impending upheaval in Eastern Europe and the Soviet Union. None of the their money, FBI, scholars and scientists could reveal to them the reaction from this Rodney King verdict. They, the powers that be, were caught off guard and will continue to be until they are removed from power by the severest of chastisements.

The Blackman and Blackwoman is as a time bomb ticking away with divine accuracy and surety that it will surely explode and not be a dud. What scares white folks more than anything is this time bomb ticking right in their very house and they are powerless to stop it. Mind you, what happened in Los Angeles and other cities is just a sneak preview of what is about to happen in just a few days.

What is setting off this bomb is the knowledge of self and the devil. Knowledge that he should "accept his own and be his self," in the words of the Most Honorable Elijah Muhammad. Knowledge that even when the devil is caught red handed with his pants down in the whorehouse of injustice, he will still deny he ever did any wrong. _Clinton on 99

Even as this beast lifts off his mask to show his true self (as The Honorable Elijah Muhammad said he would in his last days here) many of his kind are embarrassed and dissatisfied. Many were embarrassed because their true feelings were expressed without fear or shame for all the world to see with this verdict. Even as Adam (read *Before Adam the Original Man*) and his people try to cover their naked shame by calling their favorite Toms to the White House and hiring the wonder white boy (Peter Uebberoth) to appease the masses with some voluntary slave work (jobs) our people, especially the young Black men, have decided to take justice and stop waiting for it to be handed to them on a silver platter.

This is the generation; the cold, hard, liberation generation that the prophets foretold, all our ancestors prayed for and all of our open enemies dreaded would come. These are the young people, especially the men, who cannot stand the blatant lies and open destruction brought down on them by a criminal minded mis-education system. *No!* We want to get paid. We ain't down with the non-violent school. We won't take it anymore. We were instead made to *give it back* to the man who brought us here in the first place. (I guess you can tell what generation I'm from! Please forgive the slang). For all of our courage, intelligence and power, We must equip ourselves with the proper knowledge, wisdom and understanding to guide ourselves properly. This word goes out to all brothers and sisters who are putting down their guns and knives and fists against themselves and picking them up against our not 400, but 6,000 year old open enemy. This goes out to my cousin (on my Mothers' side) who I hope will find a way to read this. Due credit must also be given to gang members of all types who have settled their differences with the help of this verdict, the work of Jim Brown, the Nation of Islam members on the West Coast and ultimately Allah Himself.

First giving all thanks and praise to Allah who came in the Person of Master Fard Muhammad and who raised in our midst The Most Honorable Elijah Muhammad who left in our midst a Divine Reminder and Comforter, the Honorable Louis Farrakhan. That said. . . brothers we must have wisdom to complement our unquestionable courage. Here is a picture.

The Honorable Louis Farrakhan was once given a parable by the Most Honorable Elijah Muhammad about a bull and a lion. As the story goes, one day a bull and a lion were walking with each other when they encountered a locomotive train in their path. Well the bull snorted, got his horns pointed and charged at the locomotive. The two collided and the bull was left in a heap beside the tracks. The lion waited patiently for the train to pass by and as he passed by the bull he said, "Hummph! That's some bull." Now the point is this. Both the bull and the lion were brave without doubt, but only one had the wisdom to use that bravery properly.

Brothers, we have not the aircraft carriers and global thermal nuclear missiles to deal with this beast, but what We do have is a power that shakes up the devil right down to his yellow spine. All of the guns in world are no match for one believing man or woman. Who created in the gun in first place? Destroying and razing your own community, even if owned by equal opportunity exploiters (like the Koreans), will still not do as much good as boycotting them and spending our dollars with self.

We must defend ourselves from whoever would attack us yes, but We can't deal that ultimate death blow. That privilege belongs solely to Allah and his Christ. If you should still feel the urge to do something physical then stop your brother or sister from selling drugs to each other or more quickly killing each other. Stop the fights at the parties. Defend our elders from being robbed, beaten, raped and killed. You know what time it is. Prepare yourself and let's prepare ourselves for the ultimate conclusion of this war which begins in the mind.

. . . . . . . . . . . . . . . . . . . . . . . . . . . . . . . . . . . . . . . . . . . . . . .

**GREGORY X (Ibn. H. Khalif Khalifah)** is a 1991 Honors' graduate of Hampton University, Hampton, Va. He is the author of "Exploring the Issue of Reparations For Black People In America." He is presently working in his familys' publishing business in Tidewater, Virginia.

# GAINS & LOSSES
## In Proper Perspective
### By
# H. Khalif Khalifah

NEWPORT NEWS, VIRGINIA

At the last count the toll in the rebellion that began in the predominantly Black neighborhood in Los Angeles April 29, 1992 was: 58 dead; 18,000 arrested; about 7,000 injured with upwards of $1 billion in property damage. These figures do not include the tolls taken in lives, injuries and property damage that took place in several other cities in North America, including Toronto, Canada. The questions that all should be confronted with today is, "could it happen here? And what can, or should I be doing in preparation to survive it?"

Of course, the short answer to the first question is an unequivocal **YES!** it is more likely than not, that one day soon the Black Rebellion will engulf your city. Living on the edge, as do more Africans in America than not, few will argue with this short answer. For the pain and frustration that accompany powerlessness is etched in the faces of Black people coast to coast. *We have seen too much to ever revert back to denials that betray the reality of our slave status in the United States of America. We* have seen and experienced too much to deny the anger that wells up and burst at opportune and inopportune times in the oppressed society within which we find ourselves, victims. We have seen and experienced too much to suppress our **positive attitudes** about the rebellious activities of our people in Los Angeles, San Francisco, Las Vegas, Atlanta, Seattle, New York City, Mt. Vernon, New York, Canada, and other places where Africans took their rage to the street -- dramatizing their dissatisfaction with the blatant denial of basic human rights to Rodney King. Today our major concerns center around our efforts to solidify the gains, or benefits derived from the Los Angeles Rebellion. For we understand this is the surest way to prepare for other rebellions that are bound to follow. Maybe sooner rather than later.

## ALREADY BEEN TAUGHT WHAT TO DO TO PREPARE OURSELVES FOR THIS DAY & TIME

After the Los Angeles Rebellion, hopefully, more Africans will have seen and experienced enough to take the advice of The Honorable Elijah Muhammad and prepare ourselves for the day when the bare necessities of life will not be available in our own communities. For over forty years, Mr. Muhammad advised African people in general; and directed his own followers to prepare for the coming days of rage by saving certain food items. He told us to store dry beans, rice, flour, powered milk and other items so we could survive. He also advised us to buy farm land to grow our own foods; establish factories to manufacture needed goods, etc., & etc. Of course these are among the physical things he taught us to do to prepare. But he also taught us on no uncertain terms, that the spirituality he received directly from the God, Who came in the Person of Master Fard Muhammad, is absolutely essential for good success in all our pursuits. We all are well advised to go back to the teachings of The Honorable Elijah Muhammad to become more acquainted with everything that he taught. The fact is, one of the main reasons you are reading this book is because of a conversation that I had with a follower of the Honorable Elijah Muhammad in Los Angeles who was, in fact, prepared because he took and carried out the instructions of The Honorable Elijah Muhammad. After talking with Brother Nasir Hakim; hearing him tell about how he and his family had properly stored the food stuffs that Mr. Muhammad had told us to, I knew that somehow instructions must be given to our people -- using Los Angeles as an object lesson. The Los Angeles Rebellion will be a wake up call for the followers of the Honorable Elijah Muhammad. For many of us, self included, though we do store certain amounts of food, have not stored as seriously as we will from this time on. As far as I am concerned, the most beneficial thing to come out of the Los Angeles. Rebellion is the alarm that it sounds for those Africans who never stopped preparing or hoping for the day our people would act to take back control of our own destiny.

The removal of alien businesses that had a stranglehold on the economic life of the community is one of the major residual side benefits. Of course the most beneficial gains from a spontaneous, explosive revolt like this, will be determined as we move forward to meet the next precipitous event that will spark another rebellion. If we learn well from this one, no doubt, we will be better prepared for the next. For one thing is certain, we know that Los Angeles will be better off because of the Rodney King Rebellion. This is mainly because of the work that the conscious were already about when the rebellion began. It can mean more or less of a plus, for the community is so devastated and steeped in ignorance, despair and hopelessness, that the flexing of the muscles of the Sleeping Giant will help more than we know; especially if we (the conscious) do our work in the coming weeks.

The leaders of the African community who were engaged in activities that centered around the survival and independence needs of the Black Nation are yet to be heard from, in regards to the Los Angeles Rebellion. But even as the caucasian media brought forth one kind of traditional Black leader (integration minded) after another to analyze and comment on the rebellion, their analysis and response to the questions only magnified the words, acts and deeds of those Africans who were already telling our people what is needed; and things we should have been doing to prepare for the coming challenges to our survival, individually and as a people. Of course we vary in some ways, also, about some things that we should be doing. But the common thread that runs through this segment of the African community is the fact that whatever else we may be, the main ingredient in all our activities is the philosophy of African nationalism. We believe in self determination. As such we welcome the responsibility to do for ourselves. We ridded ourselves of dependency on anyone, other than our Creator, and ourselves, long before this day. The masters in the race during the 20th century left many undiluted records and instructions as to how to achieve all of our sovereignty and independence aspirations and goals. Masters, Marcus Garvey, Minister Malcolm X & the Honorable Elijah Muhammad, left no stone unturned, if there was anything under it that we needed to guide and protect our Nation.

## RAPARATIONS & OTHER AFRICAN NATIONALIST PROGRAMS IGNORED BUT THE PEOPLE ALREADY KNOW

For every program that Black spokesmen for President Bush, or wanna be president, Clinton or Brown proposed, there is already a clearly stated program that comes from the African nationalist perspective. When they talk about "rebuilding" we know that the best solution is for **them** *not to rebuild anything in the Black community*. This kind of thinking is the main reason for the revolt. It is also the reason there will be more and more revolts, throughout the U. S. in the coming months: *The only way that the community can be rebuilt to last, would be if it was rebuilt for the good and welfare of the Black community. And the* *only way that this can be assured is to pay our people the reparations owed for over 400 years of free and low wages in this society. Put the money required to rebuild in the hands of Africans* who demand "reparations" as the basis for all discussions with the children of the slave masters of our fore parents.

All of the reparations need not paid now, for the emergency demands immediate attention. But the principle and definite guidelines for the negotiations must be established. In other words, "X" amount of billions can be advanced, as reparations, while the negotiations continue. Of course the advanced reparations money must be used to rebuild more than the physical structures in our communities. Generally speaking, our people need a spiritual as well as physically over haul. Fortunately, we have all the professional know how, and expertise that we need. This is true, whether we're talking about reclaiming our children, healing our drug addicts, or reprogramming our uncle Toms, etc. But more importantly, it means putting our good, hard working, conscious, intelligent Black men and women in a setting where they can experience the heaven on earth that was promised by our Messenger. We can achieve, or at least begin to build towards all of these things, if our overdue reparations were factored into our budgets, as a people. Now, we do not mean to over simply the intricate nature of what must be done to achieve our freedom, justice and equality. But we do want you to get the great vision that has been laid2 out before us. We must have our just due. And yes, it all starts with the payment of our reparations (if we are discussing how caucasian people figure in our plans.

Nothing short of this kind of commitment will bring any lasting solutions. For those who would like to have a more thorough understanding of what reparations are, how we should be paid, to whom and how they will be distributed to our people, please read the little book called **Reparations, Yes!!,** By Omari Obadele, Chokwe Lumumba & Nkechi Taifa, **What Muslims Want** (the Nation of Islam program), and a new book due out this year, **Exploring the Issue of Reparations For Blacks in America,** by a young, Honor Graduate of Hampton in June, 1991, Gregory X, aka Ibn H. Khalif Khalifah.

For those who maybe fuzzy in your understanding of what reparations are, we will only take the space to share with you a simple definition: Reparations is simply the payment of a people who have been collectively abused over a period of time, or in the case of the Japanese in World War II, a specific time. ($20,000 per Japanese abused has already been allocated). When it can be proven that a people have been brutalized, in chattel slavery and subjected to other kinds of oppression, as a people, international law, and political precedents throughout history, says they are entitled to the payment of reparations by the guilty party.

Only the complete idiot, or nit wit deny that the descendents of captive Africans, that were brought to

North America, are entitled to reparations from the government of the U. S. Since there are relatively few complete idiots & nit wits, in the world, just about everyone will discuss some kinds of redress for the injustices that have visited African people over the past 500, or so centuries. The main reasons the discussions do not get to, or address main or real solutions is that up to now the caucasian rulers of America refuse to even call what they propose reparations: so discussions about justice for Black people in America comes up short because they refuse to fully address the payment of our overdue reparations.

Also, and contrary to what many Black and caucasians may think, it is not that we do not have very eloquent spokespersons who are in service to African people; committed individuals whose basic philosophy about race relations center around the payment of our reparations. The demands are, and have been unceasing throughout our enslavement. Imari Obadele, the president of the Republic of New Afrika have been in the forefront of the demand for many years. His little book, called, *"Reparations, Yes!"* is a document that has reduced our demands for reparations down to terms that will be understood by anyone. Mr. Obadele is an internationally known, historic figure in our history, but you would not know this by the character of the people that caucasian media brought forth to discuss the Los Angeles Rebellion, or to engage in serious discussions about rebuilding the city. Mr. Obadele, besides writing books (more than 10), he is also a college professor at Southern University in Texas.

Of course, the one person that should have been called upon; in fact, the main one that will have to be satisfied when serious discussions take place about our reparations, or any other programs that deal with basic, just solutions, is non other than Minister Louis Farrakhan. As the National Representative for The Honorable Elijah Muhammad, Minister Farrakhan is easily the most powerful Blackman in North America. He is the only one capable of calling qualified, disciplined, fearless Blackmen into formation overnight. His part of the Nation of Islam contains the most profound wealth of institutions and resources in the Black Nation. But we know they will try first to go around Minister Farrakhan. This will not work, for unless he is fully consulted and represented at all discussions, any discussions will simply be an exercise in futility.

In other words, it will be just as foolish to think that a permanent solution can be found for African people without Minister Farrakhans' oversight, as it is to think that a solution can be found without fully addressing the reparations rights and demands of conscious African people. So don't try it!

The Black man must retake control over his own destiny. Nothing short of complete control will do. And since we cannot expect this complete control to be given to us by the people who control our destiny for their own selfish reasons, we must rebel, again and again until our demands for freedom, justice and equality are met. So for those who condemn the leaders of the revolt, as well as the hundreds of thousands, perhaps, who participated in it, there is more, much more to come. There are things one can do to get ready. And there are things some can do to prevent them from happening. Past history tells us, and the solutions they are presenting for discussion tells us, they are going to make the same mistakes. We **must not**: so we must prepare for the worse, which means more rebellions in U. S. cities. Your city may be next.

\* \* \* \*

## LESSONS FROM THE CHATTEL SLAVERY PERIOD IN OUR HISTORY IN THE UNITED STATES OF AMERICA

As history tells us, during the chattel slavery period in the U. S. the rebellions of slaves had far reaching consequences for both the slave and the slaver. And while those who would cultivate, rewrite, or ignore real history to fit their own self interest would have us to believe otherwise, the far reaching consequences had both negative and positive sides.

For the slaves the basic negative side was the fact that his rebellion was thwarted before it could be developed into a full blown revolution; while the basic negative side for the slaver is the fact that even under the most inhuman conditions imaginable, *his slaves* still rebelled and exacted a great retribution against he and his family. And though the basic positive side for the slaver is the fact that he discovered, or checked the rebellion before the leaders of the rebellion were able to marshal enough power to engineer a successful revolution, this satisfaction is mitigated by the fact that the lives of his loved ones had been lost; of course the damage to his property may hurt more than anything else, since he is so materialistic. And while these are terrible consequences for the slaver in a slave rebellion, they pale when measured against the long term affect of a good rebellion. That is, the psychic damage to the entire slave holding population.

## LONG TERM AFFECTS TAKES THE GREATEST TOLL

Psyche is related to the usage and power of the mind. So when ones psyche is impaired he or she is in disrepair, indeed. Damage control for the psychically impaired is best achieved when the cause of the damage is kept out of sight -- out of mind. Since the cause for the damage to the slavers psyche are his own rebellious slaves, it is not possible for him to get away from the source of his mental problems, unless he goes out of the slave owning business. This he would not do. But slave revolts like Denmark Vesey's (1822 in Charleston, S. C.) and Nat Turner's ( 1831 in Southampton County, VA.) reveals on no uncertain terms the brutal, demonic mentality of the European slave holders. Besides hanging all of the warriors charged in the planned revolts, untold numbers they could not relate to any part of the revolt were rounded up and sold out of the area. And of course, the brutality did not end there. The wanton slaying of Black men continued in the area in for years afterwards.

What we are saying is that the demented mentality of the slave holder is such that paranoia commonly set in. He develops such a terrifying fear of a revolt by Black captives that he is always nervous. It got so bad during chattel slavery that these evil people even passed laws that authorized the state to compensate any slave holder whose slave was "justifiably" killed. Much of the brutality to keep the slave in subjection was driven by fear. Any careful analysis of U. S. society today, will expose this same basic fear.

As we strive to get the most we can out of the energetic revolt by African people in Los Angeles, we must not lose sight of the fact that the only things that have really changed in our relationships to the slave masters children, relative to that of their fathers to our fore parents, is the fact that the chains are on our minds, rather than physical confinement. Our status in relation to the slave masters children is absolutely the same. As such, the methods they use to try and control us are relatively the same. Their fear that one day we will revolt and kill as many of them as we can get our hands on is also the same. If we understood this better, we would better understand their release of the four cops that beat the brains out of Rodney King

(also, given his dumb statements before and after the

verdict, it appears they also beat any good sense out that he may have had in him).

The scene of the brutal beating of the truck driver during the Los Angeles Revolt was a dream coming true for many; a nightmare dream, but it is one that they have probably imagined many time. The beating of the truck driver was just one instance of the people taking vengeance against their oppressors. Regardless as to how boldly they will scape goat the four brothers arrested for beating the truck driver, the nightmare of brothers beating a caucasian, in retribution only added fear to the demented slave masters children psyche.

There were other accounts of Black people stopping motor vehicles driven by caucasians, dragging them out of cars to beat the living day light out of them. Of course one of the perplexing things about the revolt remains the sight of white people running in and out of the same stores that Black people were sacking. Why didn't the brothers and sisters attack them? This may well be a carry over from our history. Everyone acknowledges the facts about our peaceful nature. Our good nature. Even during period of our vengeance, we manage to maintain a healthy degree of our humanity.

Take the Nat Turner campaign in Southhampton County Virginia (1831), until one reads the accounts about his dynamic march through the countryside, it will appear that Ol' Nat simply killed all caucasians encountered along the way. This is not true. Nat Turner selectively killed only those caucasians who owned slaves. He marched around non slave holding caucasians to get to those who held chattel slaves. But absolutely no mercy was shown for those caucasian families that held Black people captives. One would think that this would be a source of comfort for the children of our former slave masters, but apparently it isn't. They are so afraid that we are going to try to kill as many of them as they killed of us that it interferes with their enjoyment of the benefits they enjoy from our free labor. Personally I'd be very surprised if Black people killed any more caucasians than is necessary to gain control over the situation; and you must gain control over the situation in order to get control over the destiny of African people. We will not rest until we have this control. Also, there will be no rest for anyone else until we get the control. For as Minister Malcolm X said: "Freedom for everyone, or Freedom for no one." In more words, **No Justice No peace!**

# C. R. O. E.
## Coalition For The Remembrance of Elijah (Elijah Muhammad)

## By MUNIR MUHAMMAD

IN THE NAME OF ALLAH, THE BENEFICENT,
THE MERCIFUL. I BEAR WITNESS THAT
THERE IS NO GOD BUT ALLAH AND I BEAR
WITNESS THAT ELIJAH MUHAMMAD IS HIS
LAST MESSENGER

My dear Brothers and Sisters, I begin this article by reminding us about America's historical, brutal treatment of the so-called American Negro. Initially my reaction toward the beating of Rodney King was that my people had to wake up. But now, having time to think and reassess the teachings of The Honorable Elijah Muhammad, I realize many of us will have to be killed because we continue to defend the slavemaster's actions; and the killings will go on until God Himself intervenes.

The Honorable Elijah Muhammad gave us clear cut programs, solutions to all of our problems. There aren't any European or Negro solution; there has to be a divine solution to the so-called American Negro's problem. According to the Honorable Elijah Muhammad, God appeared in the Person of Master Fard Muhammad. He began solving our problems at once.

*"Those who believe and are the doers of good, there is no fear for them nor shall they grieve,"* this was and is a reality to the believers of the teaching of The Honorable Elijah Muhammad.

As we go back in time, just a few years ago we discover that there was a similar incident to the Rodney King event in Miami, Florida. The only difference between the two situations was that the driver in Miami, Mr. McDuffie was beaten to death, but the results were the same, though evidence was stacked against them, the perpetrators were was tried for the crime and acquitted.

Before going into details about the incident in Miami, and it's relation to Rodney King, I would like to share some of the wisdom of The Honorable Elijah Muhammad. I would like for the reader's to examine this wisdom and tell me if the shoe fits today. *"The Negro leaders are frightened to death and are afraid to ask for anything other than a job. The good things of this earth could be theirs if they would only unite and acquire wealth as their slavemaster and other independent nations have.*

*"The Negroes could have all of this if they could get up and work for self. The slavemaster has given you enough education to do for self, but this education isn't being used for self. It is even offered back to the slavemasters to help them keep you a dependent people, looking to them for support. Let us unite every good that is in us for the*

uplifting of the American so-called

equality of the world's independent nat

The Honorable Elijah Muhammad ha

point program, I pray that Allah b

examine His wisdom:

*(1) Separate yourselves from the slavemaster*

*(2) Pool your resources, education and qualifications for independence.*

*(3) Stop forcing yourselves into places where you are not wanted.*

*(4) Make your own neighborhood a decent place to live.*

*(5) Rid yourselves of the lust of wine and drink and learn to love self and your kind before loving others.*

*(6) Unite to create a future for yourself.*

*(7) Build your own homes, schools, hospitals and factories.*

*(8) Do not seek to mix your blood through racial integration.*

*(9) Stop buying expensive cars, fine clothes and shoes before being able to live in a fine home.*

*(10) Spend your money among yourselves.*

*(11) Build an economic system among yourselves.*

*(12) Protect your women.*

Now let's examine the parallel between Los Angeles and Miami.

In Miami, the Black community of Overtown had been a stable one up to the late 1950's. There was forced segregation, but within the confines, Blacks were able to

lf. As far as businesses was concerned, there were
owned producers, as well as goods and services.

Many of the properties in Overtown were owned and
managed by a white land owner by the name of Luther
Brooks. In 1959 or 1960 there was a move to build an
Interstate Highway through the section of Overtown. The
highway eventually displaced about 20,000 people,
approximately 50% of the population. White land owners
and government officials conspired to take the properties
from the Blacks through imminent domain. Because Blacks
weren't involved in decision making, they were displaced
with few problems for whites, but many for themselves.
Even relocating was a major problem because the
community that they were forced to move into (Liberty
City) was predominantly white, at the time. There was an
immediate conflict.

A Black man by the name of Frank Legree attempted to
water his lawn, while whites were picketing his home.
He'd previously been threatened with death, if he did not
move out of the community. Anyway, in watering his
lawn, some of the protesting whites got wet. He was
arrested by the police. Here the Black man had been
forced to move from his own neighborhood into one
where he was not wanted. But when the Black man was
living in his own neighborhood, the white man was not
satisfied. Which just goes to illustrate perfectly that we
can't do anything to please them. The Messenger had told
us in Number 3 above, "stop forcing yourselves in to places

106

where you are not wanted." We could also add, or letting them force you. . .

In December, 1979, Liberty City was hit with the tragic killing of Arthur McDuffie, a business man, who was also an ex-Marine in the U. s. Army. Still, he was denied basic human rights.

During a night out, riding his motorcycle, he was stopped by policemen and beaten to death. But despite the confessions and testimony of Policemen, Charles Veverka and Mark Meir (who testified for the state), that they withheld evidence crucial to the case, all of the defendants were acquitted. the venue for the trial had been changed to a city where a jury of 12 white males were impaneled! Does this sound familiar?

Mr. McDuffie's murder was covered up; they attempted to make him a criminal even though he was not only very prominent in the community, he was also a long time friend of the Public Safety Spokesman. Another city official, the Deputy Medical Examiner testified that Mr. McDuffie had been beaten without mercy. So there was no doubt about the criminal acts of the police. But on May 17, 1980 they were found "not guilty!" The rest is in the history books: Black people, incensed by the verdict, burned a good part of the city of Miami. Also, like they did in Los Angeles after the Rodney King verdict, it appears that Black people suffered the most. But there were casualties on both sides. Reportedly, 10 Blacks and 7 whites were killed in a terrifying rebellion.

It was reported that many of the whites were killed in the same way some were killed and beaten in the Rodney King Rebellion; pulled from vehicles as they tried to ride through the Black neighborhoods. They *did* report almost as many whites died as Blacks. This is not the case in Los Angeles, where they admit to but two whites killed. But it is not so much the actual number that was killed, in either case, it is the fact that the Blacks were fighting back, taking a life for a life.

Also, as in Los Angeles, the terrible conditions under which Black people were living before the rebellion was *suddenly* discovered. U. S. president at the time, Jimmy Carter commissioned a group of Negroe's and Liberal whites to investigate the so-called riot. First, as recently proposed by present U. S. president, Bush, they asked for millions of dollars to restore millions of dollars in property damage.

Of course, after the glare of publicity subsided and the passage of time, the problems before the riots are just as bad or worse then they were before.

The Spokesman for the Public Safety Commission, the Black man referred to early on as the friend of Mr. McDuffie, was helpless in the pursuit of justice for his friend, even though he held a prominent position in the government. so what chance do ordinary Black people have to receive justice any place in America? God will give us justice, not the enemy of God.

108

Cases like the above have been repeated over and time again in the history of the Blackman in America. I hope that the Rodney King verdict will be the case that will really wake us up to the reality of the situation we are in. It is a situation that continually places us at the mercy of white people, the enemy of God. We will receive our justice from God, but we must wake up and do something for self, as the Honorable Elijah Muhammad taught us, over and over again.

How many more reminders we need is anyone's guess, but, programs to save ourselves and our people are available for study and implementation. The Honorable Elijah Muhammad left some very clear records. He also left some very good examples of how one will be successful, if you study and accept the formula that he left.

Many of the forecasts and warnings of our Messenger are coming true right before our eyes. For those who accepted his guidance and instructions, "there is no fear, nor will we grieve." But we are challenged to continue to point our people to the programs of The Honorable Elijah Muhammad as the solutions for all their problems. Perhaps, as the stories of the brothers and sisters in Los Angeles, who really followed the instructions of The Messenger, come out, others will see how valuable the teachings of Mr. Muhammad really are. We have already heard about one family that had stored the food stuffs that The Messenger told us to. When the grocery stores were burned down in Los Angeles, this family was not worried about at least one thing needed to survive, "What they were going to eat to live."

The Rodney King Rebellion is a reminder of the brutal beast nature of the enemy of God. Take a look at Miami, 12 years ago, then look at Los Angeles today. Then compare. Then look ahead; think of what possibly could change in the condition of Black people at the mercy of white people. Nothing will change unless we bring it about. We must do for self. We can start by being knowledgeable about the programs that are working for more successful Black men & women than you would imagine.

. . . . . . . . . . . . . . . . . . . . . . . . . . . . . . . . . . . . . . . . . . . .

**MUNIR MUHAMMAD** is the Business Manager for C.R.O.E (Coalition For the Remembrance of Elijah). C.R.O.E. is a research institution, based in Chicago, Illinois, for the works about the Honorable Elijah Muhammad. It houses, perhaps, the most extensive collection of writings, audio and video taped records in the world, by for and about The Messenger of Allah, The Honorable Elijah Muhammad. For information about C.R.O.E., 2435 W. 71st Street, Chicago, I. 60629. Or call (312) 925-1600.

# LYNCHING AND THE AMERICAN INJUSTICE SYSTEM

By
**ADIB RASHAD**
**Washington, D. C.**

The verdict reached by the jury in the Rodney King trial angered all Americans of moral conscious and, in particular, the African-American community, which for years has found itself victimized by similar judicial lynchings. And that decision which exonerated those four devils was nothing else by a contemporary lynching that has continuous historical roots. Lynching in any form is endemic to the American tradition. Historically, and in actual practice, lynching is the ultimate use of coercion against Black people to maintain white hegemony. Lynching in a racist society is nothing but a legitimate means to check the activities of the Black community.

The creator of lynching was a Quaker, Charles Lynch, a political leader of what is today Lynchburg, Virginia. During the American revolution, Lynch and his political cohorts decided to establish an extra-legal court to curb the outbreak of criminal activity. The closest court was two hundred miles away; therefore, with Lynch as the chief magistrate these frontier Caucasians took legal matters into their own hands. As a result of the success of this extra legal court, others were established in Kentucky and in the Carolinas after the revolution. Southern Caucasians upheld this so-called system of justice as honorable and as an efficient means of protecting private property (slaves).

Through the diligent and persistent work of Ida B. Wells, Walter White and the National Association for the Advancement of Colored People, the tradition of lynching was submerged and subsequently transformed into a more modern kind of brutality. Thus white racist vigilantism was replaced by the state and Federal apparatus which are equally racist and diabolical.

The police are now America's legally armed vigilantes and they maintain capitalism and racism according to the dictates of Eurocentrism. The police forces of municipal and metropolitan areas operate with impunity in their daily acts of brutality against Blacks and other non-whites. The police are like an occupying army patrolling the exploited, impoverished non-white areas, keeping the sullen population in line with excessive harassment, intimidation, and terror. Each year in almost every city in this demented nation scores of unarmed persons, mostly people of color -- especially African Americans -- are brutalized or killed by white racist police officers. It is therefore clear that the police under the state and Federal government through the criminal injustice system has become the modern instrument to perpetuate white supremacy. Hence, the extra-legal court lynchings initiated by Charles Lynch were replaced by governmental lynchings and capital punishment.

In conclusion, each of us must express outrage that an injustice was indeed rendered in the Rodney King case. Most outrageous of all is the fact that those on whom we depend for our protection -- the police and the judicial system -- are obviously the perpetrators of this gross injustice. Most African-Americans are aware of situations similar to that of Rodney King. This stems from the myth that Eurocentric America has created stereotypes which portray young Black males as violent, poor, ignorant, and criminal. Most of Euro America accepts this myth, and the police frequently enforce this view as in the case of King. This perception of young African American males, concomitant with overt and institutional racism that exists in most Euro Americans, prompts some police officers to the kinds of horrendous acts that was revealed in the Rodney King video tape.

The American government needs to be vigorously condemned for its continual illegal and legal lynchings of people of color. We must also sustain a mindful observation on the conditions that produced that justifiable disturbance in Los Angeles.

Until this unjust, hypocritical nation transforms and subsequently improves the living conditions of non-white people, and in particular African Americans or Africans who happen to involuntarily reside in the United States, the seed for further disturbances is inevitable.

. . . . . . . . . . . . . . . . . . . . . . . . . . . . . . . . . . . . . . . . . . .

**ADIB RASHAD** is the Author of *"Aspects of Euro-Centric Thought: Racism, Sexism & Imperialism"*; and *"The History of Islam and Black Nationalism in the Americas."*
He is an educational consultant, history, English, and math teacher. He also directs and teaches the curriculum for GED program. He has completed undergraduate and graduate degrees in history, philosophy, and Adult Education. He has traveled and lived in Africa, and visited parts of Eastern Europe and Southeast Asia. Mr. Rashad is a regular contributor to *The National Newport News and Commentator.*

# DARE TO STRUGGLE DARE TO WIN FREEDOM OR DEATH!

By

## AL-HAJJ IDRIS A. MUHAMMAD

## New York, New York

In the Name of Allah, the Beneficent, the Merciful
Allah the Exalted said; Oppression is worse than slaughter,
(Holy Quran).

"There are no laws that the oppressor makes that the oppressed are bound to respect." (Huey P. Newton).

An insurrection occurred in Los Angeles yesterday after four sadistic coward European KKK cops, all charged in the video taped beating of Rodney King. They are Timothy Wind, Sgt. Stacey Koon, and Theodore Briseno. The judge declared a mistrial for one cop named Lawrence Powell on one count involving the use of excessive force.

Within hours of the fake verdict, the revolt or insurrection broke out. By late last night, there were unconfirmed reports of eight deaths and three hundred people injured. Los Angeles Mayor Tom (as in uncle) Bradley who is an ex-cop and a fool, he gave the key of the city to the South African Consulate, he also is a friend to all zionist jews, an avowed enemy to Minister Farrakhan. He declared a state of emergency and Ku Klux Klan governor Pete Wilson called out the national guard.

A Los Angeles cop spokeswoman said that they didn't have enough cops to deal with the uprising which the cops falsely called a riot. We must remember what occurred in Los Angeles was an open revolt against civil authority or a constituted government. Thousands of demonstrators directed their rage at the sadistic cops outside of one of Los Angeles crack houses (precinct).

George Bush, a hypocritical lowlife dog, appealed for calm and reason in the community. There will never be calm in the Afrikan community as long as oppression exist. The recent incidents in Los Angeles are part of the continuation of a long Amerikkkan tradition of state brutality toward people of Afrikan descent in Los Angeles.

The Rodney King case began in April, 1991, when 4 cops, in the presence of several others, brutally beat motorist, Rodney King, as he lay on his stomach, or attempted to crawl away.

The attempted lynching was filmed by a neighbor who was awakened by the loud and vicious beating of Rodney King last April. If the camera hadn't caught the cops in the act, then it would have been just Kings word against 25 KKK sadistic cops. All of the cops would have been prepared to swear on a stack of bibles that King was violent and reached in his pants pocket for a weapon and had to be restrained by the cops who were acting in fear of their lives. Doubters can read the initial cop report which virtually said the same thing. This was before the video was released for public viewing and revealed the usual routine cop conspiracy and coverup about their criminal attacks and daily atrocities against Afrikan people.

The arrogant stupid comments of Darryl Gates revealed his total contempt for the Afrikan community; his belief that a man of Afrikan descent "has no rights that a European is bound to respect," (this quote is taken from a lowlife KKK Supreme court judge named Tanney in the 19th century).

The lead prosecutor in the case was Terry White 35, a man of Afrikan descent who graduated from UCLA law school. He worked on organized crime cases from 1984 until joining the Special Investigating Division that handles misconduct cases in Los Angeles last year, had never prosecuted a cop brutality case before. The first order of business for White should have been to make sure the jury would not be composed of low life KKK Europeans without some Afrikans on the jury. He did not take care of this first order; and This proved to be his most serious error. He also should have prevented the judge from changing the venue from Los Angeles to Simi Valley, which has the lowest crime rate, and more sadistic cops living there, than any other place in California. White should never have trusted these Europeans, because if a European hasn't proved to Afrikan people through many years of struggle against the KKK, cops, and other oppressive forces that they are his enemy then his own people should not trust them either.

These European fools had no intention at the beginning of this trial to convict these sadistic cops. Terry White knows now that an Afrikan can not receive justice at the hands of Europeans in the criminal injustice system. The Asian and the Chicano (on the jury) were used by the Europeans to acquit the cops. These two fools closed their eyes to oppression that is also on the heads of their own people. Europeans consider all Afrikans guilty first; and we prove ourselves innocent. Afrikan people know that the majority of Europeans are savage beasts because their history speaks for itself. We are human and they are beast and we must never compare them to us in any manner.

Justice will manifest for Afrikan people only by our hands, such as in the case of Adam Abdul-Hakeem, formerly known as Larry Davis, through self determination and self defense he was victorious in a shootout against 30 cop assassins, who tried to kill him because he exposed their cop drug ring in the Bronx, New York, which he refused to be a part of anymore, so the only way he could leave this drug ring alive, was to shoot his way out. After being acquitted in three trials, convicted on a weapons charge, (the weapons actually belonged to the corrupt cops). Given 5-15, the appeal is presently active. Railroaded into another 25 to life conviction by a cop jury, this appeal is active, framed with a fake kidnapping charge, which Adam is presently on trial for. His last trial will be for a fake prison assault. If Allah wills, he will be victorious again.

Afrikan people must establish what Allah says in the Holy Quran, "an eye for an eye and a tooth for a tooth, and a life for a life." When the cops and other oppressive forces in this country realize that they may have to pay with their lives when they kill Afrikan men, women and children, the killings will stop.

When the Black Liberation Army was active in the five boroughs in New York City, killings by sadistic cops of Afrikan people were minuscule, because these soldiers practice what Allah, the Creator says in the Holy Quran, retaliation is prescribed for those who believe in Allah, his prophet and the last day.

*Dare to Struggle, Dare to Win, Freedom or Death.*

. . . . . . . . . . . . . . . . . . . . . . . . . . . . . . . . . . . . . . . . . . . . . .

**AL-HAJJ IDRIS A. MUHAMMAD** lives in New York City. He is the co-Founder of the Adam Abdul-Hakeem Defense Committee; and is the author of a book called: *What to do If You Are Arrested or Framed by The Cops.*

# AMERICA THE BRUTIFUL!!

## By

## MINISTER NEAL N. JACKSON
## (Bro. Ahmad N. Jakim)

## Richmond, Virginia

In 1955 in the state of Mississippi a young Black (African) youth was found dead in the bottom of a creek. It was the body of fourteen year old Emmitt Till. He had been lynched, shot, stabbed, and mutilated at the hands of a racist white mob who claimed he whistled at a white woman. This was only one of the "hundreds" of murders afflicted upon Black youth's in 1955 that fell in the hands of the media.

In 1959 the state of Mississippi once again focused on the death of a young Black man. Twenty-three year old Mack Parker was lynched at the hands of (so-called) "God-fearing" white men. All over the nation the media publicized the brutal death of yet another Black man.

But it did not stop here! In Birmingham, Alabama, in 1963, four young 'beautiful' Black girls were killed in the Sixteenth Street Baptist Church. Addie Mae Collins, Carol Robertson, Carol D. McNair, and Cynthia Wesley were attending their Sunday school class when a bomb that was thrown into the church exploded, killing the four girls instantly.

Yes, for the Black man and woman in America the slogan, "America the Beautiful" is nothing more than "America the Brutiful." Brutality is the philosophy of the American society when dealing with her Black (African) citizens. We know that it was American-brutality that motivated the killing of Black Panther Chairman Fred Hampton on December 4, 1969. It was the same brutality that killed Yusef Hawkins and many other young men and women of African descent.

And now! in 1992, we have seen the 1991 video tape beating of a Black man in Los Angeles, California at the hands of four white racist policemen who were freed of all charges of police brutality by a predominantly white jury, in an all white community.

Rodney King was hit over 50 times within the 81 seconds of the video taping. Not only was this Black man beaten physically, but he was also beaten mentally. White politicians and lawyers brutally attacked the mind of brother Rodney King, persuading him to foolishly stand before a "brutal" and "racist" society, making such a statement that all people (Black & white) must stay calm and learn to love each other.

Does not Rodney King know that he represents hundreds of Black men and women who are brutally beaten and killed daily by white-americans?

Does he not understand that this so-called "Rodney King incident" is beyond him?....that the anger of Black people is not flamed from the beating that he took, but more so from what his beating means to Black people as a whole?

How can you teach the brother or sister of an Emmitt Till to love the man who lynched their beloved brother ? How are we ever to expect the mother's of the four little sister's killed in a church, on a Sunday morning, to pray for the men who killed their innocent daughters?

If America truly wishes to stop the violence in the nation, then it must be stopped first by destroying her racial attitudes towards Black people and all people of color. Until so, Black people must unite and plan so that there won't be any more Rodney King beatings. There shall be times when we (Blacks) must accept the fact that violence must be met with violence. We must come to realize that if we keep "turning the other cheek" we soon won't have a cheek to turn. African (Black) people are being brutally beaten and killed all over the world. Rodney King's beating is nothing new, it just fell into the hands of the news media who saw it as a chance for capital gain. These Euro -American(s) cared nothing for the man who was beaten by the four racist policemen, but only for the money they would get for airing the video tape from their television stations before any others.

The beating of our brother Rodney King was a visual warning to all Black people! It does not matter whether you are Christian or Muslim, Democratic or Republican, the white man see's you as the same. . ."a nigger!" And the faster we get that message in our minds the better off we shall be.

This is the time and the hour for unification. . . well, to be totally honest it is far past time. Nevertheless, we must move with all the force and power that we have!

The message is out! The gangs are unifying, the non-violent Black leaders are now angry, so if you are not willing to die for your freedom; then move out of the way! And as they say, "Get the hell outta Dodge" cause there's a new warrior on the warpath and he's taking no prisoners!

# THE 'NEW WORLD ORDER'
# &
# THE RODNEY KING VERDICT

## By Gloria Taylor Edwards

## Richmond, Va.

I. *The Problem:* In March, 1991 people everywhere proclaimed shock as the videotaped vicious beating of a New Afrikan man by four European policemen while fifteen other police looked on, was blazoned across the visual monitors and airways of America. Other New Afrikans waited months to see the outcome of what everyone seemed to think would be some form of justice for Rodney King, and ultimately all people of color. Now, more than one year later, and after a verdict wielded from a Simi Valley, California courtroom which turned Los Angeles inside out for nearly three days, the nation suddenly seems to have awakened itself from an amnesiac sleep and wants to re-examine its age-old 'Negro problem'.

This writer has listened, read, and viewed New Afrikans, other people of color, and Europeans assessments of the aftermath of the Rodney King verdict. One particular comment made in my presence by a European who proclaims sympathy for the economic and social conditions of the Rodney Kings of America was, "Why--why the burning and beatings? Don't most Black people know that we were just as shocked and appalled by the verdict? Don't most of you believe what Dr. King emphasized, that "two wrongs don't make a right'? A quiet march or something--but why beat up other people who may be on your side, and burn up businesses, including Black businesses? Why?"

As the European shook her head while concluding her feelings, I decided to address her comments. I reminded her of the first, and only words, Rodney King has said publicly since his entire ordeal. Those words were, " Can-can we all get along?"

I continued, more to the New Afrikans who were also present while the European was talking, and were now agreeing with her or shaking their heads in confusion, "That's been the problem every since the Afrikan captives set foot here in the 'new world'. While I feel connected to my New Afrikan brother, Rodney King's words made me just as sad as watching the L.A. riot on television. Always-always we are asked to either forgive, forget, overlook, or passively address things... and usually we wind up doing all, or one those things. But until New Afrikans take collective and constructive action against the problem there will be many more reoccurrences of Rodney King's beatings, as well as the verdict. And the problem is not small-time criminals, as Rodney King has been labeled...the problem is not so called 'Black on Black' crime, drug abuse, poverty, or hopelessness and despair. The problem is WHITE SUPREMACY. . .and everything else previously said are symptoms. Not until we address the problem will the symptoms go away. Since Rosa Parks in 1955, eventually Dr. King and the whole civil rights movement, America has attempted to calm the masses with her 'band-aid' remedies by voting every ten years or so, since 1967, on a civil rights bill, or waging a 'war on poverty' that was already too little and too late and just in time for the economy to begin to fall apart in 1973."

"Can we all get along?" Brother Rodney King asked? I say that most of us would be very happy if that were possible at this time in history. But for the practitioners of White Supremacy, the world power mongers, and greedy corporate America, it would not fit their plans right now for us all to get along. The 'new world order' which Mr. Bush has spoken of alleges to promote world unity and peace. But there is no justice in America, and it is America who proposes to lead this 'new world order.' And though the participants in the Los Angeles rebellion accomplished nothing in their random and violent actions, the words they chanted were very ominous. . ."No Justice, No Peace." So, the answer is no to Brother Rodney King. We cannot get along. . .not until we address the problem of White Supremacy."

By then my European conversant had paled and was beginning to back away from the group as if she was in shock. I had not raised my voice or my right fist in a 'Black Power' sign, and I couldn't understand why she should have appeared so frightened. Anyway, I gathered I'd said enough for the group of people there, so I also walked away. This was one New Afrikan sister who had work to do. I had no more time to explain, much less excuse or apologize for anything said by myself which I felt promoted a truthful look at the problem.

II. A FIRST-HAND CASE SCENARIO:  I was a first-time offender, convicted on worthless check charges and given 41/2 in 1981. Two months were spent in a jail setting in Richmond, Virginia, and additional time was spent in the Goochland Correctional Center for Women in Goochland County, Virginia. I gained trustee status in both settings, was the first New Afrikan female inmate to serve as secretary to the assistant warden in Goochland, and obtained a college-level Business diploma while incarcerated. I was paroled my first time up, (June, 1982), after having served nearly one year.

The horror that I lived, and the aftermath, has made me to know that I have to 'proclaim' evil revealed to me, as well as the hidden message surrounding my evolution process during this traumatic time in my life.  In my semi-fact based autobiography, *The Proclamation,* which is due to be released in June, 1992, I tell my full story.

I have selected the following passage from *The Proclamation* to give some insight on my personal experience.

". . .I saw and learned things I could never have experienced from books or television. . .and I paid the penalty of finding out the reality of life from the other side of the prison bars.

"Anger, fear, suspicion, vindictiveness, paranoia, and hostility are the major emotions displayed in such a setting. It became a way of life for me, too. My heart felt something cold continuing to grow. However, it all reinforced one thought to me, rehabilitation comes from within and not from being in an institution. For when you cage or lock up any free-moving being, after a short period of time, they react just as caged animals. . .they become beings existing on the lower elements of their senses, moving along by simple instinct. . .survival at any cost. . .kill or be killed. And there is more than one way to kill a person, the quickest is to kill the body. But the most effective way to control any free-will thinking Beings, though, is to kill the mind and let the body live on. . ."

III. THE ANALYSIS: a) How do we relate the overall fight for liberation of all Afrikan/New Afrikan people to Rodney King's beating, and the court's verdict of that beating? Afrikan, New Afrikans, and *all* people of color need to look at the whole picture.

Law and order, what does it really mean to the practitioners of White Supremacy?

The beating of Rodney King was not an isolated incident, and neither was the verdict. Police brutality is as old as the lynchings of the early 1900's. Some seem to have forgotten the 1980 civil rights investigation of the fatal beating of New Afrikan motorist Arthur McDuffie by European officers in Miami, Florida. Here, four officers were acquitted and there was subsequent *rioting* in Miami. Video taped or not, where was the conscious of America for McDuffie's family's ordeal? What was, and still is so significant about Rodney King's beating?

The trial of the officers who beat Rodney King was moved from an ethnically diverse Los Angeles to a predominantly white suburb called Simi Valley. Out of 400 jury prospects only six were New Afrikans. Only two New Afrikans made it to the jury box, and the defense attorneys had those two removed through challenges. No prosecutor, attorneys for Rodney King, judge, or whoever, did anything to aggressively challenge this. It was a kangaroo court in its most blatant form.

But American idealists *had to see* for themselves that justice *is not* blind in America. In a nation where New Afrikans make up approximately 13% of the population, they contribute a whopping 41.7% of the prison population. . .stats say the figures are still climbing.

Rodney King's ordeal did two major things. One, on the positive side it served as a wake-up call to many New Afrikans in America. However, on the negative side, this

THE RODNEY KING VERDICT & THE NEW WORLD ORDER

writer is of the opinion that Rodney King's beating and verdict served as a test maneuvered by white supremacists and the power mongers to allow them to see what it would take to escalate a race war, and to see how far it could go before the masses could accept instituting martial law.

"A bold statement of opinion," some may say, and "reeking in paranoia," others may add. But this writer will go even further and say that the conspirators are preparing the stage to be just right for their 'new world order,' and they are willing to sacrifice even a few of their own to initiate their master plan. This Master Plan for their 'new world order' will ultimately lead to 'one-world' rule. b) Now, what exactly does white supremacy mean? What is meant by 'new world order' when voiced by today's powers-that-be?

Neely Fuller, Jr., in his book *The United Independent Code/System/Concept: a Textbook/Workbook for Thought, Speech, And/Or Action for Victims of Racism (White Supremacy)*, defines White Supremacy as *(1) "the direct or indirect subjugation of all non-white people by White people, for the basic purpose of pleasing and/or serving any or all White persons, at all times, in all places, in all areas of activity, including economics, education, entertainment, labor, law, politics, religion, sex and war; (2) the only functional Racism in existence that is based on color and/or anti-color in the physical make-up or physical appearance of persons."*

A recent survey reveals that New Afrikans and Europeans

differ on what integration means. 'Whites' idea of integration is one Black to every fifteen whites with a white person in control, while Blacks tend to think of ideal integration on a 50-50 Black-White ratio with a Black, or White, in control.

One need not be a rocket scientist to understand that if most Europeans feel this way in 1992, it's quite unlikely they are going to change their feelings of superiority any time soon, if ever.

The phrase 'new world' order has certainly been banded about, sometimes rather loosely, for many centuries.

'New world' is described in the World Book Encyclopedia as another name for the Western Hemisphere which includes the continents of North and South America. For those who are interested, the World Book Encyclopedia defines the Eastern Hemisphere as the 'old world,' and the 'old world' includes the continents of Europe, Asia, Africa and Australia.

Today's powers-that-be have been using the phrase 'new world order' a great deal lately.

In an article printed in the Arizona Daily Star on January 3, 1989, a headline written by the Associated Press read, "Millenium Groups Expects Bush at '99 Egypt Bash." The article reported that organizers of the Millenium Society had solicited the presence of Mr. Bush and his wife for a celebration in Egypt at the Great Pyramids of Cheops in Giza, in 1999. Mr. Bush accepted.

The following is an excerpt from a speech delivered by

George Bush. The date is March 16, 1989 and he is now president. He said, "What are we doing to prepare ourselves for the new world coming just 11 short years from now?"

The question should be, what are New Afrikans doing to prepare ourselves for this 'new world' Mr. Bush is speaking of? Mr. Bush expects to attend a celebration to usher in 2000. Will the majority of New Afrikan people have much to celebrate by the end of this year; much less the year 2000?

The headlines of a commentary by writer John Hall which appeared in a Richmond, Virginia newspaper dated April 11, 1991, boldly read "Bush Quiet on New World Order."

Memory for most of us here in America should flashback to early 1991 when Mr. Bush make his flippant 'read my hips' statement, which seemed more like 'kiss my butt,' if you think about it. So, can New Afrikans afford to gamble on what's going to be done to equate justice out to ourselves: What kind of people could endure the continued injustices of White Supremacy this long and not have severe social and economic problems? As things stand right now, how much more do we need to see before we realize, "ain't no Easter Bunnies, ain't no kindlier, America," nor our children's children should forgive us if we don't wake up with some remedies that do not include waiting for a miracle to drop out of the sky -- or, at least out of Washington, anyway.

133

## HOW DO WE TIE IT ALL TOGETHER
## FOR SOME SOLUTIONS?

The Rodney King beating and verdict was a symptom, amid many symptoms, that we are in a broken society that is out of control. So, how can a 'system' responsible for protecting society and rehabilitating offenders, reflect the conscious of a 'civilized' and free world when its continued practice of White Supremacy is lawless within itself?

A 'new world order' with old business as usual is what the White Supremacists are aiming for. Those who propose to move forward, whether analyzing Rodney King's ordeal or not, must look candidly at the sins of America which encompasses thousands and thousands of injustices that have never been acknowledged openly, much less rectified. America has a history of conspiracy to conceal the TRUTH ABOUT her injustices against humankind.

It's not a matter of anti-patriotism. . .it's a matter of JUSTICE, RIGHTEOUSNESS, and BALANCE. The laws of Karma teaches us the rules of the Universe, which literally means 'what goes around comes around,' or 'what you put out you get back.'

There may be some who may argue, then, that Rodney King was a two bit criminal who provoked the law and therefore received back what he put out. Keeping that same mind-set, let's list the crimes which America has committed. When the thirteen little colonies was developed to become what they later named America, American history has 'pretended' that a new world were discovered whose land previously belonged to no one else.

134

These colonists robbed from, murdered, ravaged and seized properties from the indigenous Red Man. Then they kidnaped, terrorized and brutalized Afrikan captives into physical bondage and built their new country's wealth on stolen land and slave labor. After further robbing the Afrikan captives descendants of inheritance rights from their parents' forced labor, now the children of that Mayflower pilgrimage brag and promote their country, at home and abroad, as the 'land of milk and honey' and where everyone can pursue the American dream of capitalism. America presents herself, up to this point in history, as the foremost promoter of democracy in the 'new world,' and worthy to lead the world in global peace. Her crimes, thus far, are grand-master theft and double-major larceny, mass murder, aggravated rape and lewdness, acts of war, abduction, inhumane treatment of all people of color, fraud, and impersonating a democracy.

So, just when will America get back what she has put out, as some would say Rodney King did? And, for that matter, who constitutes America? If America was truly a democracy, the masses would constitute the governings of America. But she is not a true democracy. . .so, just 'who' should be responsible for her criminal acts then?

POWER is the name of what controls the strings of America, and almost the entire world systems. In this piece POWER is an acronym which stands for Persons of Woeful Evil and Rancor, and consists of those behind Global 2000, along with the world's international bankers, for they

## THE NEW WORLD ORDER & THE RODNEY KING

control the monies and the oil. These individuals in POWER are maliciously plotting the destruction of the misfits, those classified as down-breeders, and all free thinkers. Those left after Global 2000 will be those whom POWER consider the most 'physically capable' for living in their 'new world order' . . . a created society.

POWER shall be responsible for America's and their other global, criminal deeds. At the risk of sounding spookish to some, this writer believes that since POWER are not just two-bit criminals, but universal and master law breakers, the laws of Karma says their punishment shall come back from the Universe. Therefore, those of us who propose to be on the side of Justice better stand back and be sure to not align ourselves with these entities. . .for they shall be made to destroy themselves and will be taking anything and everybody that ain't nailed down in TRUTH, RIGHTEOUSNESS, and BALANCE with them.

'Way out,' some may say -- 'sci-fi,' others may say. For further clarification, valuable solutions and remedies, this writer suggests reading the book by Terrance Jackson, *Putting It All Together,* published by U. B. & U. S. Communications Systems, 1991, Hampton, Va. This writer has never met Brother Jackson, but scanning and reading his works, and 'putting it all together' from other resources, strongly recommends that New Afrikans read his work, and then research for themselves.

## WHERE DO WE GO FROM HERE?

It would be foolish to map out specific strategies in this written piece. Raising consciousness about POWER must be done carefully. The individuals and entities behind POWER are powerful, and therefore dangerous. If this writer, and others like myself, who are saying these seemingly way-out, unpatriotic things, suddenly are gone for some unexplained reason, those who want a better tomorrow *must* continue the work. Plus, 'they' are aware that we are in the eleventh hour and approaching five minutes before midnight, therefore, they must work before the 'warriors' for a righteous human existence can alert others of their evil purposes. POWER struggles daily to divide people by continuing to create and manipulate world events, as well as the media.

For some immediate suggestions: the first thing we should do when some of us come together is develop a Co-op project with a health food store, or start our own, so that we can afford to stop feeding ourselves and our children crap that's killing our brain cells and our bodies. Then, while we're cleaning ourselves up inside, we should carry our children to libraries, bookstores, and places where they can continuously learn new things. We should encourage settings which emphasize spiritual enlighten-ment, reading, discussions, self-esteem, motivation, and sharing among New Afrikan children -- we must not allow our children to become conditioned to a 'rote' form of learning, so we must stimulate creativity and resourcefulness in them. As best we can, we should support organizations, businesses, churches, and individuals who are actively working for the betterment of our future. If we can not do it with money, lend them our hands and our minds. Finally, we must Love, and dedicate all future efforts for a better tomorrow to our children. We should teach them to love, justice, truth, and righteousness. We should, as much as we possibly can, Love ourselves and each other. To do as much of the things suggested here for ourselves and our children is vital, because we will still be showing them a better way to love by taking care of one's body, soul and mind. . .that life should, and will be better for them. It can be done.

If we should begin a commitment this day to our children and ourselves before this Global 2000 fully overtakes most of us, instead of a 'new world order' we can celebrate a 'just world order.'

. . . . . . . . . . . . . . . . . . . . . . . . . . . . . . . . . . . . . . . . . . . . . . . .
**Gloria Taylor Edwards** is an education/cultural consultant for New Afrikan children, a freelance writer, and author of The Great Awakening series, and The Proclamation.

# RECOMMENDED READING LIST

THE THEOLOGY OF TIME, By The Honorable Elijah Muhammad   $24.95 complete book (600 pages) $10.95 Book 1

**Stolen Legacy, By George G. M. James** ...   **13.95/19.95hb**

Aspects of Euro-Centric Thought, By Adib Rashad .   13.95

**Bumpy Johnson/Lumumba Odingo:** TWO UNCOMPROMISED BLACK-MEN IN THE SLAVERY SOCIETY CALLED THE UNITED STATES OF AMERICA .. **7.95**

Yakub & Origins of White Supremacy:MTWM ....   11.95

**The Auto-Bio of Malcolm X, By Alex Haley** ........   **5.96**

Profusion: Analysis & Commentary on The Blackman's Guide to Understanding the Blackman, By Khalifah   5.95

**Isis Papers, By Dr. Frances C. Welsing** ............   **14.95**

Blackman's Guide to Understanding the Blackman By Sister Shahrazad Ali .........................   10.00

**Blackwoman's Guide to Understanding the Blackman By Sister Shahrazad Ali** ......................   **10.00**

Destruction of Black Civilization, By C. Williams ...   16.95

**Visions For Black Men, By Na'im Akbar** ..........   **8.95**

They Stole It But You Must Return It, By R. Williams   9.95

**The Philosophy & Opinions of Marcus Garvey** ....   **10.95**

Race First, By Dr. Tony Martin ...................   10.95

**The Power of Thought, By Kendryck Allen** ........   **8.95**

The Jacobite Scheme, By Abass Rassoull ..........   6.95

Message to the Blackman, By T. H. Elijah Muhammad   10.

African Fables, By Dr. Linus A. Bassey .............   6.95

Musa: The All Seeing Eye, By Prince A. Cuba .......   6.96

The True History of Jesus, By T H. Elijah Muhammad   6.95

Culture Bandits, By Del Jones ...................   10.95

Words From An Unchained Mind, By S. Whitehurst   10.00

Queen Hatshepsut, By Prof. John F. Hatchett ......   5.95

Capoeira: African/Brazilian Karete, By Y. A. Salaam   5.95

Black Exodus, By Ahmad Jakim .................   10.95

Heru (Comic Books) I II & III, By Roger Barnes .   $3. & 2.50

Freedom, Justice & Equality, By Greg Parks ........   4.95

How Beautiful De Swatches, By Marva Cooper .....   3.95

Apartheid: The Untold Story, By Corbin Seavers ...   5.95

Servants of Power, By Charles Powell ........ H. B. 18.95
Safe Sex in Age of A.I.D.S., By Curtis Cost .......... 4.95
The Art of Dread locks, By Wanda Johnson ........ 4.50
Black Parents Handbook for Ed. Children, Baruti ... 5.95
100 Amazing Facts About the Negro, By J. A. Rogers 3.95
5 Negro Presidents, By J. A. Rogers .............. 2.95
Putting It All Together, By Terrance Jackson ....... 7.95
Mis-Education of the Negro, By Carter G. Woodson 9.95
Back Where We Belong, By Joseph Eure ......... 13.95
A Healthy Nutrition Handbook, By Keith Wright ... 8.95
Iceman Inheritance, By Michael Bradley .......... 15.95
Black Muslims in America, By C. Eric Lincoln ...... 14.95
My Soliloquy, By Leah J. Reynolds ............... 5.95
Am I Asking Too Much, By Gwendolyn Tait-Dover . 6.95
A Black Angel Delivers A Message, By L. Pinckney .. 6.95
Struggle, By Shelomi ........................... 5.95
Who Is The New Afrikan?, By Zolo Agona Azania .. 3.95
Hey Dummy, By Lonnie Clinkscale ............... 5.96
...................................................
...................................................

U. B. & U. S. COMMUNICATIONS SYSTEMS
1040-D Settlers Landing Rd. ● Hampton, Va. 23669
1-804-723-2696 ........... Fax Number (804) 728-1554

# BUMPY JOHNSON
(Charleston, S.C., 10/31/06 - 7/7/68) &

# LUMUMBA ODINGO
(Charleston, S.C., 6/6/18, --------)

By
Lumumba Odingo & H. Khalif Khalifah

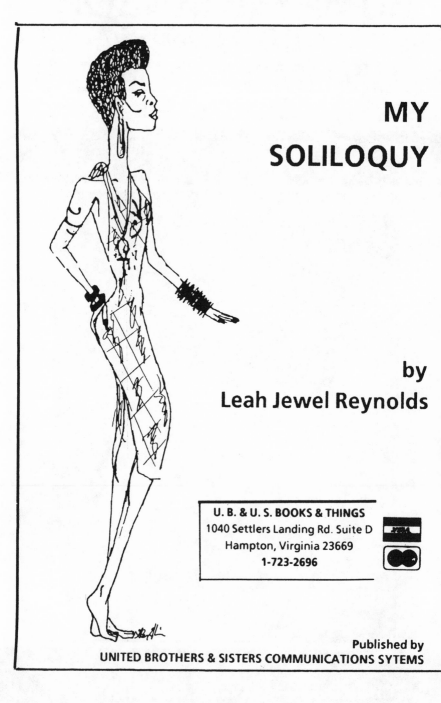

# MY
# SOLILOQUY

by
## Leah Jewel Reynolds

**U. B. & U. S. BOOKS & THINGS**
1040 Settlers Landing Rd. Suite D
Hampton, Virginia 23669
**1-723-2696**

Published by
**UNITED BROTHERS & SISTERS COMMUNICATIONS SYTEMS**

**Profusion** by H. K. Khalifah is an analysis and commentary on the economic, social and literary impact of the Blackman's Guide to Understanding the Blackwoman.

Khalifah's analysis takes a deeper look into the minds of the men and women whose reactions to Sharazad Ali's book resulted a monumental achievement in the Black literary marketplace in the U.S.

**U. B. & U. S. BOOKS & THINGS**
1040 Settlers Landing Rd Suite D
Hampton, Virginia 23669
**1-723-2696**

## PROFUSION:

**WHATEVER ONE MAY THINK OF IT:**
Analysis & Commentary on the
Economic, Social & Literary Impact of

THE

**BLACKMAN'S**

GUIDE

**TO UNDERSTANDING**

THE

**BLACKWOMAN**

ON THE NATIONAL AFRICAN COMMUNITY

By

**H. Khalif Khalifah**

PUBLISHED BY UNITED BROTHERS & UNITED SISTERS
COMMUNICATIONS SYSTEMS

# UNITED BROTHERS

# &

# UNITED SISTERS

# COMMUNICATIONS SYSTEMS

1040 Settlers Landing Road Suite D
Hampton, Virginia 23669
1-804-723-2696 (telephone) (804) 728-1554 (fax #)

# ●PUBLISHERS

# ●PRINTERS

# ●DISTRIBUTORS

Providing All Your Present and Future
Information Needs VIA The Printed Word